Ulysses S. Grant

18th President of the United States

Lucille Falkof

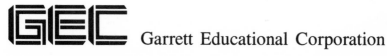 Garrett Educational Corporation

Manufactured in the United States of America

Edited and produced by Synthegraphics Corporation

Library of Congress Cataloging in Publication Data

Falkof, Lucille, 1924–
   Ulysses S. Grant, 18th President of the United States.

   (Presidents of the United States)
   Bibliography: p.
   Includes index.
   Summary: Follows the life of the Civil War general
and president from birth to death, examining his child-
hood, education, employment, and political career.
   1. Grant, Ulysses S. (Ulysses Simpson), 1822–1885 –
Juvenile literature.   2. Presidents – United States –
Biography – Juvenile literature. [1. Grant, Ulysses S.
(Ulysses Simpson), 1822–1885.   2. Presidents]
I. Title.   II. Series.
E672.F22   1988   973.8'2'0924   [B]   [92]   87-32817
ISBN 0-944483-02-X

Contents

Chronology for Ulysses S. Grant

1822   Born on April 27

1843   Graduated United States Military Academy at West Point

1845–1848   Served in Mexican-American War

1848   Married Julia Dent, August 12

1853   Resigned from United States Army

1861–1865   Served in Civil War

1861   Appointed Colonel for 21st Illinois Volunteers

1863   Won battle of Vicksburg; appointed major-general in regular army

1864   Became supreme commander of the Union armies

1865   Lee surrendered at Appomattox, April 9

1867   Appointed interim secretary of war by President Andrew Johnson

1869–1877   Served as 18th President of the United States

1877–1879   Toured the world

1880   Lost Republican nomination for a third term

1884–1885   Wrote *Memoirs*

1885   Died on July 23

Chapter 1

What's in a Name?

For just a moment, the 17-year-old hesitated. Entering the United States Military Academy at West Point, New York, was a big enough step. But changing one's name? What would his father say to that!

Sucking in his breath, he drew himself to his full five feet one and approached the officer at the desk. Before he could explain, the officer barked, "Sign here!"

The young man crouched over the desk and carefully scratched out, "Ulysses Hiram Grant." There, it was done. Without telling his father, he had switched the first and second names. By doing so, he would never again be embarrassed by his initials. He remembered how unhappy he had been when the elegant new trunk for his West Point journey had arrived. There, outlined in shiny brass tacks, were the letters "H.U.G."

The officer slowly moved his finger down the list and shook his head.

"Sorry, young man, I have no one by that name on my roster. The only Grant from Ohio is a Ulysses Simpson Grant."

Ulysses winced. Why had they used his mother's maiden name as his middle name? He was to learn later that the congressman who had obtained his appointment to West Point had forgotten his official name. He remembered only that the boy had been called "Ulysses," and then inserted the maiden name of Ulysses' mother.

When the young man tried to explain, he was told in a firm voice that the only way the change could be made was by an order from the War Department. Without further protest, Ulysses took the register and signed as requested.

But his "new name" day was not yet over. The names of all the newcomers had been posted on the bulletin board. Ulysses was listed as "U.S. Grant." As the cadets crowded around the board, they started making up new names for the initials. Among them were "United States Grant" and "Uncle Sam Grant." Then, when they saw the short, round-faced boy and compared him to the tall, strong cartoon character—the symbol of America—they laughed even more. "Uncle Sam" gradually was shortened to just plain "Sam." Years later, Civil War generals who had attended West Point with Grant would greet him as "Sam Grant."

For Ulysses, his name had always been a burden. It was a month after his birth before the family could agree on what to call him. Grandpa Simpson liked "Hiram." Both his father and Grandma Simpson favored "Ulysses," the great hero of the Trojan Wars. After much debate, the names were put into a hat. The first one chosen was "Hiram," the second one, "Ulysses." Though Hiram Ulysses may have been his official name, the real one is what your mother calls you. Hannah Simpson Grant called her son "Ulysses," or "Lyss" for short.

FAMILY ROOTS

Born on April 27, 1822, in Point Pleasant, Ohio, Ulysses was the oldest of Jesse and Hannah Grant's six children. Jesse Grant could trace his ancestry back to Matthew Grant, who sailed from Plymouth, England, to Dorchester, Massachusetts in 1630. Five years later, Matthew moved to Windsor, Connecticut, where he served for 40 years as the colony's surveyor. Jesse's grandfather was killed while serving under the British in the French and Indian Wars. Jesse's father, Noah Grant, joined the Continental Army and served in the Revolutionary War from the battle of Bunker Hill to the final victory at Yorktown. After the war, he left Connecticut and settled in Ohio in 1799.

Jesse and Hannah Grant

Jesse Grant was a tanner by trade. He was a proud and outspoken man who had been on his own since he was 11 years old. By the time he married Hannah Simpson in 1821, he was part owner of a tannery in Point Pleasant. Two years later, he moved with Hannah and one-year-old Ulysses to Georgetown, Ohio, where he had his own tannery.

Hannah Simpson Grant was a shy and deeply religious woman of few words. She said little beyond "Yes" or "No," but when she spoke, it was usually in a calm, measured voice that assured others that all was well with her husband, her children . . . and the world.

SCHOOL DAYS

At age five, Ulysses started school. Because there were no free schools at that time, his parents paid a small fee for him to attend classes in a one-room schoolhouse. In his autobiography, Ulysses noted that there were as many as 30 to 40 students in the room, ranging in age from five to 20 years old.

Ulysses was an average student whose only special talent seemed to be in arithmetic. Although he was an obedient student, he occasionally earned a beating with birch branch switches from his male teacher.

Education was very important to Ulysses' father. When Ulysses was 15 years old, his father sent him to a private boarding academy for two winters, perhaps in hopes of preparing him for West Point. But the school did not offer much more than the one-room school in his hometown.

A photograph of Hannah and Jesse Grant, parents of Ulysses Grant. (Library of Congress.)

The years in Georgetown were happy ones for Ulysses. As he grew older, however, he seemed more and more to take on the shyness of his mother. Perhaps he was becoming more sensitive to his father's boastful talk around the town. For Jesse Grant had made it known, almost from the time Ulysses was born, that his son was a "genius." Jesse might have been a great political debater (he was a co-founder of the Georgetown Debating Society), but his son would have none of it. Ulysses hated arguments and especially any form of public speaking. Ulysses also made it known that he did not like the tanning trade and did not plan to follow in his father's footsteps. Surprisingly enough, this did not anger Jesse. He realized that Ulysses had other interests.

"LYSS" EARNS HIS SPURS

To Hannah Grant's neighbors, her quiet manner often seemed strange. When Lyss was only three or four, he would crawl beneath the bellies of the horses in the family stable, or he would swing on the tails of strange horses tied to hitching posts in the center of town. When the neighbors rushed excitedly to Hannah with the news, she simply smiled and replied, "Oh, I don't worry about Lyss. He has a way with horses." And he did.

From his earliest years, Lyss was neither awed by the size of horses nor frightened by their unpredictable movement. Early on, Jesse allowed Ulysses to ride the work horses twice a day down to the creek for water. By age five, he could be seen standing on the backs of the horses, holding the reins and balancing himself like a circus performer.

Ulysses had the opportunity to act like a performer when the one-ring circus came to town. He could not resist the dare when the ringmaster called out, "Is there anyone here brave enough to ride this pony?" Although the horse was trained to rear and pitch, to stop suddenly, and to try to unhorse the rider, this did not faze Ulysses. The townspeople got used to waiting for the event, and they cheered when Ulysses held on and earned what was then a large amount of money—five dollars.

By the time he was nine, Ulysses had learned to ride so well that local farmers called on him to "break" their new horses or teach them to pace. He would jump astride a bucking, tossing colt, seize the mane, and ride through the village or fields until the horse tired and became tame.

Businessman and Horse Trader

When Jesse added a livery stable to his tannery business, Ulysses was 10 years old. Jesse confidently turned over much of the stable work to Ulysses. Sometimes people objected to being put into the hands of such a small boy, but Jesse would dismiss their concerns with a casual, "Oh, he can take care of himself."

During those days, Ulysses drove passengers and goods through much of Ohio and Kentucky, to places as far away as Cincinnati. He once drove two lawyers more than 250 miles, clear across the state to Toledo. Ulysses loved the work and the opportunity to see faraway places.

Jesse was convinced that his son had a good head for business. Didn't he always try to obtain return fares whenever he delivered passengers or goods? Much later in life, however, others would seriously question Ulysses' business ability. Perhaps a story that Grant told about himself reveals a different side.

When only eight years old, Ulysses begged his father to purchase a particular colt to which he had become much attached. The farmer who owned the colt, a Mr. Ralston, had asked 25 dollars for it. Jesse thought it was worth only 20. After much pleading, Jesse finally agreed to let Ulysses try to buy the horse. But he gave him precise instructions as to how to drive a hard bargain.

Ulysses rode up to the Ralston farm. As soon as he met the farmer, he blurted out, "Papa says I am to offer you 20 dollars for the colt. If you don't take that, I am to offer $22.50. And if you don't take that, I'm to give you the 25 dollars." Mr. Ralston pocketed the 25, Ulysses took the colt, and the story had the local townspeople chuckling for weeks.

COLLEGE AT WEST POINT

As proud as Jesse Grant was of his son's skills as a horseman and businessman, he had far greater ambitions for him. He wanted Ulysses to have a college education. But finances in the Grant family were a bit tight. Two more sons and a daughter had been added to the family. Jesse's business expenses were increasing. Prices were falling and the national economy was in a state of panic. With Jesse's finances in such a poor condition, West Point seemed a logical college for Ulysses.

First of all, the education at the United States Military Academy was free. Second, there was a growing need for businessmen trained in mathematics, and the building of new roads and canals created a greater demand for engineers. West Point offered highly rated courses in both fields. Third, more than half of the graduates resigned from military life as soon as their five-year term of enlistment was completed. Ulysses did not have any great affection for military life, but with such training, other career opportunities would be open to him.

Without consulting his son, Jesse applied to Senator Thomas Morris for an appointment to West Point for Ulysses. When Jesse notified his son that he had received the appointment, Ulysses told his father that he would not go. In his memoirs, Grant describes his father's reaction. "He said he thought I would, *and I thought so too, if he did.*"

When Ulysses departed for West Point, he did not expect to be gone for long, for he knew that, once there, he had to pass a qualifying examination. Always enthralled by the prospect of a journey to new places, he relished the trip eastward. From Ripley, Ohio, he embarked upon a three-day steamboat ride to Pittsburgh. He then took a canalboat trip to Harrisburg, where he saw a railroad train for the first time and marvelled as he rode at the top speed of 18 miles an hour to Philadelphia. After he dallied for several days in both Philadelphia and New York to see the sights, he reported none too happily to West Point. It was the end of May 1839.

Examination day proved to be far less intimidating than Ulysses had anticipated. He was asked to do little more than some spelling, reading, writing, and arithmetic. With this hurdle successfully out of the way, Ulysses was now eligible to purchase his first uniform. In his expense book, he listed the following:

Swallow-tailed sheep's gray coat	$10.88
Gigtop hat	2.44
White pantaloons	10.50 per dozen

In a letter to his relatives, Ulysses described the pants as "tight to my skin as the bark to tree, and if I do not walk military— that is, if I bend over quickly or run—they are very apt to crack with a report as loud as a pistol."

Life as a Cadet

Ulysses managed to adapt himself well both to the regimen of the academy and to the strict discipline enforced upon the cadets. Not that he did not earn his fair share of demerits for such infractions as bringing food into his room or sneaking into his friends' rooms to visit after taps was blown. And there were days, especially during the long, cold winter, when he yearned to be astride a favorite colt, racing through the Ohio woodlands.

There was no doubt in his mind that he was not cut out for the military life. Ulysses detested the constant barrage of barking orders: "Suck in your guts," "Pull in that chin," "Straighten up!"

For a brief while, during his first winter at West Point, his hopes for an early return to Georgetown bloomed. A bill was introduced in Congress calling for the abolition of the military college. Many people, especially in the frontier states, believed that there was no need for such an elitest institution. In case of war, enough red-blooded men could be called to defend the country. So his hopes of an early return home were dashed when the bill, after much debate, failed to pass.

College Has Its Ups and Downs

His sophomore year marked a change for the better. Now "Sam" Grant was no longer a lowly first classman, a plebe, subject to the demands of the upperclassmen. Also, his one great passion would at last be fulfilled, for a course in horsemanship and cavalry drill was added to the formal curriculum.

This was also the year when Ulysses made the top section in mathematics. It was generally recognized that sophomore mathematics was the toughest course of all, for it included analytical geometry, calculus, and surveying. His grades in mathematics far excelled those in other areas of study. Like most people, Ulysses did best in the subjects he liked.

The sophomore year also brought about an improvement in a cadet's social life, for he was permitted to attend dances. Ulysses had the rolling gait of a horseman and such a poor sense of rhythm that he stood out like a waddling bear in the crisp line of cadets marching through the much-detested parade drills. Yet, his September accounts listed, "Dancing Master, $2.00; Cotillion parties, $2.26."

Following the second year, cadets were permitted their first furlough, or leave of absence, to go home. Only now, Ulysses would be going to a new family home. The leather business was improving, so Jesse Grant decided to expand his operations. He went into partnership with a Mr. E. A. Collins of Bethel, a nearby town, and moved the family there. Mr. Collins had opened a retail leather store in Galena, Illinois, a booming lead-mining town on the Mississippi River. Ulysses' younger brother, Simpson, now 18 years old, worked part-time in the Galena shop.

The reunion was a happy one. His mother, usually so reserved, could not resist exclaiming to her son, "My, you've grown so much straighter."

For Ulysses, it was probably the happiest summer of his life. There were young ladies who favored him with their company on long horseback rides in the countryside. He visited with old school chums. And for 10 weeks, he was free of the rat-a-tat of drums and military commands. When the time came for his return to West Point for his junior year, Ulysses was loathe to go.

Yet, there were his new friends at the Academy and the hope that he might be appointed a cadet sergeant. He had failed to make corporal in his sophomore year, so he was pleased to see his name listed among 17 other candidates. Sadly, he was again passed over and this time resigned himself to the role of "born private."

Ulysses had made up his mind to pursue a career in mathematics, hoping that upon graduation or shortly after, he might be invited back to "the Point" as an instructor in that subject. However, math was not to be offered again until the senior year so, in the meantime, he studied science and found himself intrigued by such topics as magnetism, electricity, and optics.

During his West Point years, "Sam" Grant met several young men who would touch his life again in the future, during the bitter years of the Civil War. Some, such as William Tecumseh Sherman and George McClellan, would serve with him in the armies of the North. Others who served the Confederacy, such as Thomas "Stonewall" Jackson, he would face as the enemy. Grant's quiet observations of these men — of their habits, their strengths, their weaknesses — would enable him to make sound judgments when dealing with them during the war.

During those years, the political scene outside West Point was heating up. Inside, however, boys from southern plantations, young men from northeastern cities, and homespun lads from the western states were quite friendly toward each other. But political discussions were forbidden by the authorities — and for good reason. One story holds that a fight almost erupted as a result of such a discussion between Grant and his roommate in his senior year, Fred Dent, who was to be his future brother-in-law. The boys supposedly stripped for a fight, but Sam, looking upon the ridiculous situation, suddenly burst out laughing . . . and the air cleared.

A Spectacular Finish

If Sam Grant was remembered for any outstanding achievements during his four years at West Point, it was probably for his horsemanship. For those who were present at the Class of 1843 graduation exercise, one of the most memorable events was the demonstration in the riding hall. Before an audience of elegantly dressed visitors and dignitaries, the cadets, in full uniform, put their steeds through their paces. With swords flashing, they wheeled their horses in formation and ended the maneuvers with each man hurdling over a bar set in the center of the hall. As they finished their jumps, the cadets formed two lines along the side, leaving the center clear.

The audience grew silent as the riding master strode to the center of the tanbark floor. He lifted the jumping bar higher than his head, set it firmly in place, faced the audience and bellowed, "Cadet Grant!"

From one end of the great hall galloped the slender, little cadet astride York, the most powerful stallion in the stable. Ulysses had now grown to his full manhood stature of five feet seven but he weighed only 117 pounds, the same weight as when he entered West Point. He seemed much too small and light to control such a beast.

At the other end of the hall, he wheeled York around. He gripped hard with his knees and gave the great horse his head. York thundered down the center of the arena and, in one gigantic leap, hurdled the bar. For Sam Grant, it was indeed an appropriate climax to his years at West Point.

All that remained after graduation was finding out to which branch of service each cadet would be assigned. (In the final class standing, Ulysses ranked 21 among 39.) His first choice was, of course, the cavalry—the Dragoons. His second choice was the Fourth Infantry. He went home for the summer to rest and await the news. By late July, he learned that he had, despite his fine display of horsemanship, been assigned to the infantry. He wrote to the post tailor at West Point and ordered the uniform of a second lieutenant in the Fourth Infantry.

When his new outfit finally arrived, Ulysses put it on and, striding proudly around Bethel, enjoyed admiring glances from both sexes. But as he himself later admitted, he soon had the conceit knocked out of him when several days later he saw the old stable man for the local tavern dressed in a pair of sky-blue pantaloons with a strip of cotton sheeting sewed down the outside seams—an almost perfect copy of his own uniform! From then on, Sam Grant would be more than a little skeptical about outward appearances.

Chapter 2

Love, War, and Hard Times

With the exception of horseback riding, Ulysses was a slow starter at everything he tried—including romance.

It was late September when he made his farewells to his family and reported to Jefferson Barracks. The post, situated on the outskirts of St. Louis, Missouri, offered an impressive setting for a first assignment. From the large parade ground, one could see on three sides the whitewashed limestone quarters of the officers' quarters. There was a large hall where the officers held their dances, 10 acres of gardens, and, most important to Ulysses, miles of bridle paths running through woods and fields.

The young ladies of St. Louis enjoyed the company of the post's handsomely uniformed young officers. It might be difficult to get married on a second lieutenant's salary of 64 dollars a month, but there was no doubt that romance flourished in the atmosphere around the barracks.

Lieutenant Grant hardly seemed to notice. An important priority was writing to Professor Church, his former mathematics instructor at West Point. Professor Church was optimistic that there would be a place at the Academy for Ulysses—that it was just a matter of time before a vacancy arose. This was just the incentive Ulysses needed. For the first time in his life, he was studying because he wanted to. He reviewed his old mathematics texts, began reading historical works, and even occasionally picked up a novel. He would be prepared when the opening came.

MEET JULIA DENT

One day late that fall, Ulysses remembered that he had promised his former roommate, Fred Dent, to visit White Haven, the Dent family home. It was a large but charming two-story white house. Behind it were barns, stables, and slave quarters. The Dent family made Ulysses feel very welcome.

Frederick Dent, Sr., a handsome white-haired gentleman, was the picture of a southern planter. Seated in a rocking chair on his front veranda, he loved to talk politics, and he saved his most unkind words for the northern abolitionists or anyone else who opposed slavery. For Ulysses, this was quite a change after four years in a place were politics was a forbidden subject.

Mrs. Dent immediately took to the quiet officer, as did the youngest member of the family, little Emmy, age seven. During the following months, Ulysses heard much about a 17-year-old sister, Julia, who had just finished her schooling and was visiting relatives. By the time Julia came home in February, Ulysses had established himself as a family friend who visited White Haven twice a week and often stayed for supper.

When he first saw her, Ulysses could well understand why everyone had called her "father's favorite." She was a good-looking young woman of medium height with chestnut hair and a rosy complexion. At first, Julia treated Ulysses as just another of her brother's friends who came to call at the family home. But when he discovered that Julia was a fine horsewoman, everything changed. Julia and Ulysses

This photograph of Lieutenant Ulysses Grant, as a member of the United States Army, Fourth Infantry, was taken just before he left to serve in the Mexican-American War. (Library of Congress.)

began to take long rides together, always accompanied by a fellow officer, a brother, or little Emmy. By spring, the pair could be seen riding alone, and Julia became a "regular" at the officers' balls, usually arriving on the arm of young Lieutenant Grant. However, national events were soon to quicken the pace of this leisurely romance.

IMPENDING WAR WITH MEXICO

Since the early days of the Republic, Texas was a virtually uninhabited piece of land that belonged to Mexico. But by 1820 cotton had become the most important crop in the South, and interest in Texas began to grow. Because cotton fields in the southeastern states were fast being depleted, planters needed new lands and saw the Mexican territory as a place in which to expand.

With permission from the Mexican government, immigrants from the United States flooded the area. Most continued to own and use slaves, despite the fact that slavery was explicitly forbidden by the Mexican Constitution. By 1836, Texas had been so thoroughly colonized by American immigrants that they set up their own government and declared Texas an independent nation—the Lone Star Republic. The government of Mexico refused to recognize the new nation.

For many Americans, winning Texas' independence from Mexico was only a means to several more important ends. Some saw the annexation of Texas as a way to increase the nation's land and wealth. Was it not the destiny of the United States to reach from the Atlantic to the Pacific? Others—particularly those in the South—hoped to annex Texas and make four or five states from the territory. That would increase the number of pro-slavery senators and representatives in Congress. Still others saw the annexation of Texas as a ploy to extend the evils of slavery to another part of the United States.

According to the Constitution of the United States, approval of two-thirds of the Senate was required before a territory could become a state. Though hotly debated throughout 1844, when the Texas annexation issue finally came up for a vote, it failed to pass. Then, on March 1, 1845, a bill to annex Texas did pass the Senate, though only by a *simple* majority. Because this action was both high-handed and totally unconstitutional, war between the United States and Mexico seemed inevitable.

A Time for Farewells

Anxious to see his family before going off to war, Ulysses asked for and received a 20-day leave from Jefferson Barracks. His steamer had barely cleared the boat landing when orders came for the Fourth Infantry to go south. Getting word in Bethel, Ulysses suddenly realized that he could not go south without stopping at White Haven and seeing Julia once more. He cut his leave short and raced back to Jefferson Barracks.

Lieutenant Ewell, the officer in charge at Jefferson Barracks, was sympathetic to the love-sick young man and gave him permission to go to White Haven. Reaching the local creek, Grant saw that heavy rains had turned it into a roaring river and was tempted to turn back. Yet he did not because he could not; for once Ulysses had decided on a destination, he would let nothing stop him from reaching it. Even as a driver of his father's teams, he would forge ahead – sometimes at great risk to himself and others – rather than retrace his steps. This time was no different. Besides, Julia was on the other side of the fast-moving current!

He arrived at the Dent home looking like a drowned scarecrow. Amid much laughter, the Dent family once more offered their southern hospitality. Julia's warm welcome gave him courage to blurt out what was on his mind.

But he need not have worried. For when Ulysses told Julia of his love and his hopes that she become his wife, Julia confessed her own feelings. "Only after you left did I realize how sad I'd be without you," she said.

Because she was still only 17 years old, Julia preferred a lengthy engagement. Ulysses thought otherwise. But both knew they would have a hard time gaining the approval of Colonel Dent. He had more than once commented that the hard life and long separations, which were the lot of an army wife, were not meant for his delicate daughter. Moreover, he was not sure that a northerner would make a suitable mate for the daughter of a slave-owning southerner. They decided to keep their engagement a secret.

When Ulysses boarded the steamer to join his regiment in New Orleans, the young lovers had high hopes for an early reunion. But war was to keep them apart for four long years.

THE MEXICAN-AMERICAN WAR

Lieutenant Grant served honorably throughout the Mexican-American War, but he had strong reservations about the war itself. He believed that the so-called "Army of Observation" was in fact sent to Texas to provoke a war. He later wrote, "I regard [this] war as one of the most unjust ever waged by a stronger against a weaker nation."

Grant's first combat experiences during the Mexican-American War were to provide him with two strikingly different models of how a general should look and act. The first was "Old Fuss and Feathers," General Winfield Scott. When General Scott reviewed the cadets at West Point when Grant was there, Grant had been impressed by the general's elegant bearing and manners, and by his splendid uniform.

The second model was "Old Rough and Ready," Zachary Taylor, who was a professional soldier, though not a graduate of West Point. Taylor relished action and had little use for military formality. When reviewing troops, he would often chew tobacco while sitting side-saddle on his horse. When in battle, he wore a pair of blue jeans and a floppy straw hat. Both Scott and Taylor had earned fine reputations in the War of 1812.

In New Orleans, Grant came under Taylor's command and, in the summer following the annexation of Texas, sailed with the general's forces to Corpus Christi, Texas, an old smugglers' station near the mouth of the Nueces River.

Texans insisted that the lower boundary of their territory was the Rio Grande River. Mexicans, assuming they were to recognize the state's independence (which they did not), argued that the boundary was the Nueces River. The disputed area was about the size of Massachusetts and Connecticut— and as yet uncolonized. During the fall of 1845, Grant often escorted wagon trains carrying supplies into the area. He saw no Texans and only an occasional Mexican squatter.

The United States Provokes an Attack

Despite American troop movements into the area, Mexico took no action. To win the support of Congress, President Polk knew Mexico had to attack the United States first: that a situation had to be created in which the Mexicans would be provoked to declare war. In February 1846, Polk ordered Taylor to proceed to a site across the Rio Grande River from the Mexican town of Matamoros. Polk's excuse was that the Mexican government had for the third time broken its promise to negotiate the border.

At Matamoros, Taylor established a small fort and left a small contingent of men to guard it. He then proceeded with most of his troops to Port Isabel, a supply base about 25 miles north, where reinforcements as well as ammunition and food could be brought in by boat.

In early May, U.S. soldiers at Port Isabel heard the distant rumble of cannon fire coming from the fort at Matamoros.

Learning that the Mexicans had attacked, Taylor quickly rushed his army to the scene. Until he actually saw the glittering metal lances of the Mexican army and the Mexican troops arrayed before him, Grant had been firmly convinced that a battle would not take place.

Firing began at two o'clock and continued until sunset. The action took place on a large plain, called Palo Alto, where the grass was as high as a man's shoulder. It was a battle between newly developed field artillery, rather than one of hand-to-hand combat. By sunset, the Mexicans had been routed.

By midsummer, the Mexicans had withdrawn to the Sierra Madres mountains, with Taylor's men in hot pursuit. Grant had been assigned as quartermaster, which gave him the responsibility for seeing that adequate food, ammunition, and equipment were on hand. His job also involved organizing and directing the wagon trains and pack mules. Though Grant was noted for being a gentleman who never resorted to foul language, he later spoke of being strongly tempted to swear by his experiences with the mules.

Grant to the Rescue

At one point during the battle of Palo Alto, Grant managed to find his old regiment. Their attack had bogged down, and they were running short of ammunition. Someone was needed to penetrate battle lines and inform headquarters of the situation. Grant volunteered. Riding Indian fashion, with one arm clutched around the horse's neck and his body slung to the sheltered side, Grant urged his horse forward. He arrived at headquarters unscathed and delivered the message.

Despite U.S. victories at Palo Alto and elsewhere, the Mexicans showed no inclination to surrender. But Taylor's successes had made him a national hero, and President Polk began to worry that the general's popularity might make him a presidential candidate. To deflect attention from Taylor, Polk agreed to let General Scott try his plan to attack Mexico through the port of Vera Cruz. In March 1847, Grant was present when Scott's army took the city.

Scott's next goal was to reach the heart of the country, Mexico City, which was 260 miles into the interior. To do so meant an arduous march over treacherous mountains. And to prevent heavy losses from illness, the march had to begin before the yellow fever season. (In the course of the war, more men would become sick or would die of strange fevers and diseases than would be killed in battle.)

Another Act of Bravery

Grant distinguished himself in the final storming of Mexico City. Seeing an opening in the battle lines, he led his men to a church. There, he managed to drag a light cannon up to the belfry. From this vantage point, he kept up a steady barrage of fire against the enemy. The action received enough attention for Grant to achieve the wartime rank of captain. Another hero of the Mexico City campaign was Captain Robert E. Lee. Later, during the Civil War, Lee would lead the Southern forces against Grant and the North.

During the war, Grant's job as quartermaster under General Scott taught him two important lessons about fighting a war. One was that an army without supplies cannot be effective. The second was that there are times when troops must cut loose from their supply lines and live off the land. In Mexico, at times, soldiers had been forced to forage for their own food and local people pressed into providing shoes and clothing.

Something else impressed Grant about the Mexican campaign: it was the kind and generous attitude which both Scott and Taylor displayed to the local people following each conquest. Whenever possible, Grant noted, troops were held accountable for their behavior toward Mexican civilians.

It took almost a year after the final victory at Mexico City before Ulysses returned to the United States. During those months, he had much time to think about his future. He knew his first stop would be St. Louis to see Julia. But, having lost touch with his former professor, he had long since given up his dream of becoming a mathematics instructor. Now, his only hope of supporting a wife lay in the $1,000-a-year salary he would receive as a first lieutenant, his new rank in the peacetime army.

REUNION AND WEDDING

It was a bronzed and seasoned 26-year-old who presented himself at White Haven. The Dent family and Julia in particular were elated to see Ulysses. What's more, Colonel Dent had completely overcome any earlier reservations he had about his daughter's fiancé.

There would be no question of waiting. Julia promptly set the wedding date for August 22, 1848, giving Ulysses just enough time for a brief visit home. His mother greeted him in her usual undemonstrative way, and Jesse Grant proudly showed off his son, the hero, to all the neighbors. Though neither of Ulysses' parents attended the wedding, Jesse no longer objected to the fact that Ulysses was marrying into a slave-holding, Democratic family.

On their honeymoon trip, Ulysses brought Julia home to meet Jesse and Hannah, who were so charmed with their son's lovely bride that they asked her to stay with them in case the army sent Ulysses away. The newlyweds enjoyed a memorable two months before Lieutenant Grant was ordered to report to Detroit in November 1848.

DUTY CALLS

1848! Zachary Taylor, "Old Rough and Ready," wins the presidency. Gold is discovered in California. Europeans, disgusted with war and rebellion in their native lands, hear that the United States now has one-third more territory open to settlement. Germans, Italians, Irish, and people of many other nationalities flood the ports of entry on the Atlantic coast.

To Julia and "Lyss," all of this seemed far away. On arriving in Detroit, the newlyweds learned that Ulysses had been assigned to Madison Barracks, a bleak village on the shores of Lake Ontario. By the time word reached them that there was an opening for quartermaster in Detroit, the ice and cold prevented them from getting there until the spring thaw. Julia, left without slaves for the first time in her life, managed to do the housekeeping and even to entertain in their cramped quarters. Her charm and good nature warmed not only Ulysses, but other young officers at this frigid outpost as well.

By spring, they had moved to Detroit and were much involved in the parties, fancy-dress balls, and horse-racing that made up life in the peacetime army of 8,000 soldiers. Without the excitement of marches and battles, Grant found the job of quartermaster boring. He once jokingly remarked about his work, "I was no clerk, nor had I the capacity to become one. The only place I ever found in my life to put a piece of paper so as to find it again was either a coat pocket or the hands of a clerk . . . more careful than myself."

In May of 1850, Julia presented Ulysses with his first son, Frederick Dent Grant. Despite the boredom of his work and reassignment to the Madison Barracks, life for Ulysses and Julia was fulfilling. They were looking forward to the arrival of a second child when, in the spring of 1852, the Fourth Regiment was ordered to California. In her condition, there was no way Julia could make the arduous trip, which included crossing Panama through the jungles. Because it would be at least a year before she could follow Ulysses, he thought seriously of resigning from the army. But with a wife and two children to support, his only security was his army pay. So when Ulysses' regiment left, Julia and little Frederick went to Bethel to stay with Hannah and Jesse Grant.

Through the Jungles of Panama

It was just as well that Julia and Frederick stayed in Bethel because the trip across Panama was a nightmare. From New York, the troops went by steamboat to a small port on the east coast of Panama. They then took a train for only 20 miles, after which all passengers were transported up-river in dug-out canoes. At the little town of Cruces, the War Department had arranged for mules to help the travellers make the 25-mile overland trek to the Pacific coast. As quartermaster, Grant was responsible for seeing that the troops, their families, and their belongings arrived safely at the coast.

But the person who had contracted with the War Department to supply the mules had rented them to men who were rushing to the California gold fields and who had offered to pay much higher prices. Ulysses ordered the regiment's soldiers to proceed on foot through the thick mud. In desperation, he rounded up local Indians to carry the women and children in hammocks through the treacherous terrain. Then cholera struck.

The survivors of that harrowing experience remembered Grant during those terrible days. He seemed to be everywhere, comforting women and children, nursing the sick, and burying the dead. By the time the regiment was loaded onto boats for the journey up the Pacific coast to San Francisco, more than 100 men had died.

In San Francisco, the Fourth Regiment lingered long enough for Grant to see the effect of "gold fever." Prices were so inflated that a cook was paid far more than an army captain. Even when the regiment finally settled in at the wilderness outpost of Fort Vancouver, near where the city of Portland, Oregon, is today, Grant lived with several other officers to reduce expenses. They all soon realized that if they wanted to send money home for their families, they had to find ways to supplement their army pay.

BUSINESS VENTURES AND FAILURES

For almost two years, Grant and his fellow officers tried one venture after another to raise additional funds. In letters home to Julia, he reported on each financial venture . . . and each subsequent disaster.

When the officers heard that ice was scarce in San Francisco, they had 100 tons of it cut from the river and shipped south — only to find prices greatly reduced because a fleet of ice ships arrived from Alaska at the same time. When they bought chickens and chartered a boat to ship them south, all died on route. Because prices for produce were so high, Grant and his fellow officers planted potatoes with their own hands. But just before the harvest, the Columbia River flooded the area and killed most of the crop.

As the months went by, Grant's loneliness grew. He had never seen his second son, Ulysses S. Grant, Jr., and Julia's letters about little Fred's antics only added to his longings. He hungered for news of his family, but the mail took forever to arrive.

Grant was then promoted to captain and transferred to Humboldt Bay in California. No longer a quartermaster, he found the work of a line officer even more routine and unexciting. Day by day, he became more despondent over his financial losses, and his letters home became increasingly depressed.

Forced to Resign

It was not unusual for officers who did not have their families with them to while away the hours drinking. Whisky was cheap and sold by the keg or the gallon. To attract customers, many local grocery stores kept a keg of whisky on the counter, and a tin cup attached to the spigot made it easy to have "one for the road." Free whisky was also a traditional part of political rallies and other public events. Grant, alas, succumbed to temptation.

Under the best of circumstances, Grant did not hold his liquor well. Fellow officers who knew him well commented, "With Grant, a little whisky went a long way."

One day, word leaked out that Captain Grant had been drinking. When Colonel Buchanan, Grant's commanding officer (a man with whom he'd had a run-in years earlier), heard the news, he gave Grant two options: to stand trial or to resign. Though his fellow officers assured him that he would be easily acquitted at a trial, Grant chose to resign. "I would not for all the world have my wife know that I had been tried on such a charge," he later wrote. His resignation was dated April 11, 1854.

By then his finances were in such bad shape that he was forced to borrow money from an officer friend, Simon Buckner, to pay a hotel bill while returning home. And his father sent him funds so that he could rejoin his family. No one knows what took place when Grant arrived in Bethel. No doubt, Jesse took his son's disgrace hard. He even tried unsuccessfully to get political friends to persuade the War Department to cancel Grant's resignation. Because the situation in Bethel was so bad, Ulysses left for White Haven as quickly as he could.

Grant Tries Farming

The reunion with his family lifted Grant's spirits, and it did not take long for the two boys to become adoring fans of their doting father. The family lived at White Haven while Ulysses cleared the 60 acres of land Julia's father gave her as a wedding present. There were occasional arguments with Colonel Dent over his pro-slavery stand, though Ulysses did let Julia keep the few household slaves her father had given her.

It took two years for Grant to complete the log house he built for his family. By the time they moved in, their third child, daughter Nellie, had arrived. (Years later, Nellie would come down the aisle on the arm of her father at her wedding in the White House.)

Grant dubbed his home "Hardscrabble." Perhaps the name conveyed some of his feelings at that time. Perhaps it also was his way of making fun of the fancy names the Dent family members gave their homes.

In order to make ends meet until the crops could produce enough money, Grant supported his family by cutting and hauling firewood to St. Louis. Dressed in his old blue army coat, he became a familiar sight to his customers. On more than one occasion, he would be greeted by old army friends passing through St. Louis.

An officer who had not seen Grant since their Mexican-American War days was surprised by his appearance. Seeing Grant driving a wagonload of wood, he called out, "For heavens sakes, Grant, what are you doing?" To which Ulysses, in his honest, forthright manner, replied, "I am solving the problem of poverty."

Grant was not alone among former army officers who were having financial difficulties. William Sherman left army life to enter the investment business. And when that failed, he, like Grant, joined his wife's family, hopeful of finding a solution to his problems.

Hard Times Continue

Julia Grant's mother died in 1857. Afterwards, Colonel Dent moved to St. Louis, leaving Grant to farm White Haven. To do so, however, Grant had to rent Hardscrabble. But again, his luck was bad. The Panic of 1857 struck a few months later, and bad weather destroyed any chances of a good wheat crop. Nevertheless, there was one happy event: in February 1858, the Grants had a third son, named after his "Northern" grandfather, Jesse Root Grant, Jr.

Just when the effects of the panic seemed to be over, little Fred came down with typhoid, Julia became ill with fever, and for six months, Ulysses was in and out of bed, suffering with a bout of malaria. With the help of a slave given to him by Colonel Dent, Ulysses struggled to maintain his fields and his cordwood business, but these, too, eventually failed. He was then forced to sell Hardscrabble and move to a rented cottage in St. Louis.

Grant tried the real estate business when that market seemed destined for a boom, but he could not meet expenses. He also lost out on an appointment as a county engineer because he was not affiliated with the right political party. It seemed that everything he tried was destined for failure.

THE TANNING BUSINESS—AFTER ALL

There was now nothing left for Grant to do but admit defeat and seek work in the despised tannery business. Luckily, his father needed him to work at the retail store in Galena rather than at the tannery itself.

Galena was a booming mining town on the Mississippi River. In March 1859, Ulysses moved his family there and began working with his two brothers. That same month, he freed the slave Colonel Dent had given him. Desperately in need of cash at the time, he could have auctioned off the slave, William Jones, at the current market price of $1,000. Grant never gave a reason for not doing so.

There is no doubt that Grant was becoming more and more apprehensive about what was happening in the country. He avidly read the Lincoln/Douglas debates. For Grant, the primary issue was not slavery, but maintaining the union.

To Democrats, such as Colonel Dent, Grant's freeing of his slave and his antislavery comments made Grant a Republican. To his ardently antislavery father and brothers, Grant's refusal to champion the northern cause made him a Democrat. And the one time he had voted, hadn't Ulysses voted for James Buchanan, a Democrat, because he feared that a Republican victory would push the South into secession?

Grant was a man without a party, left only with a grave concern as the radicals on both sides pressed the country towards civil war.

Chapter 3
A Nation Calls

T he sky was black and starless. Looking up at the crest of Galena's hill from the river below, the town was ablaze with lights. Flags hung in front-parlor windows, and the sound of raucous singing echoed in the cold night air. The town was in a jubilant mood that November evening in 1860.

In the Grant leather goods store, raw oysters and hard liquor rewarded the faithful Republicans who had come to celebrate Abraham Lincoln's election victory. Two men stood apart, quietly observing the delirious celebrants. One was Ulysses Grant. The other was John Rawlins, one of the town's bright young trial lawyers. A man of great charm and enthusiasm, Rawlins had earlier managed to break through Grant's natural reserve by asking him to recall his days in the Mexican-American War.

Rawlins, an outspoken supporter of Stephen Douglas, was heartened by the result of the election despite his candidate's defeat. Lincoln had 40% of the vote; Douglas 30%. John C. Breckenridge, the candidate of the Ultras, a radical southern group, had only 12%. The border states, such as Kansas and Missouri, had voted down extension of slavery into their states.

Rawlins turned to Grant. "Surely with such an overwhelming victory, the South will not continue to try and leave the Union."

Grant replied sadly, "The South will secede. The South will fight. Make no mistake about that."

Within six months, Grant's grim assessment would turn into reality. It had been long in coming—almost 70 years, in fact—but to Grant and others, a civil war now seemed inevitable.

THE "PECULIAR INSTITUTION"

Years earlier, the framers of the Constitution believed slavery to be dying out. It did not seem worth delaying the Constitutional Convention of 1789 to debate what appeared to be a minor issue. And well slavery might have died out if, just four years later, Eli Whitney had not invented the cotton gin.

Before the cotton gin, the raising of cotton was not a very profitable business. Too much slave labor was needed for the tedious task of separating he cotton from the seeds. The new machine could do the work of many slaves quickly and efficiently. Now, slaves could be used out in the fields to grow cotton, and more acreage could be planted. Cotton became the most profitable, most important crop in the South . . . and the value of slaves increased as well.

As cotton-raising developed in the South, the use of machinery and cheap immigrant labor enabled the North to develop manufacturing and trade. Although southern cotton was sold in England, the South's best customers were the mills in New England. The South also depended on the North for many of its manufactured products and consumer goods, such as textiles and iron.

Any criticism by northerners of slavery, the South's "peculiar institution," had always angered southerners. After all, they argued, racial prejudice existed in the North, where there had been little enthusiasm for the abolitionists until the 1850s. Following the Mexican-American War, however, the issue of whether a state should be slave or free once more erupted—but with greater urgency than in 1789. Political leaders debated the problem and were forced to take a stand. The South threatened secession, and with Lincoln's election to the presidency, that threat became a reality.

THE SOUTH SECEDES

The first state to secede was South Carolina—in December 1860—followed by Mississippi, Florida, Alabama, Georgia, and Texas. The secessionist states formed a new government, the Confederate States of America, with Jefferson Davis as President. Still the North took no action. Then, on April 15, 1861, Confederate troops fired on Union troops at Fort Sumter, South Carolina! The Civil War had begun. President Lincoln called for 75,000 volunteers to serve for 90 days.

That April night, the townspeople gathered at the courthouse in Galena. Patriotic fervor hung in the air. The first speaker was Congressman Elihu Washburne. Then John Rawlins stode to the platform. The audience listened in hushed silence as his words filled the room. His final words rang out, "I have favored every honorable compromise, but the day for compromise is passed. Only one course is left. We will stand by the flag of our country and appeal to the God of battle."

Among those stirred by Rawlins' words was Ulysses Grant. That night, he told his brother Orvil, "I was educated by the government and if my knowledge and experience can be of any service, I think I ought to offer them."

Grant took action immediately, scouring the area to recruit volunteers. When the quota of a hundred men was assembled and the time came to elect officers, Grant was first choice for captain. Though he agreed to train the men, he refused the position. Perhaps realizing that there would be a need for trained officers with his skill and experience, he hoped for a higher rank. Grant knew that men with no military experience were pulling political strings and being given ranks of captain, major, and colonel.

With the help of friends, Grant was offered a position in Springfield, Illinois, by Governor Richard Yates. It turned out to be routine work, consisting of everything from filling out army forms to mustering volunteers. Grant wrote to the War Department, offering his services, but the letter was misplaced. He also visited the headquarters of General George McClellan, a friend from West Point, with whom he had served in the Mexican-American War. He hoped to serve on the general's staff, but after two days of waiting to see McClellan, he left.

A Call to Serve

Returning to Galena, Grant found a telegram from Governor Yates, offering him the rank of colonel in the Seventh District Regiment. It was 90 days after the President's first call to arms, and now Lincoln was seeking three-year enlistment terms. The young farm boys who comprised the Seventh Regiment despised their drunken commander. They had already rebelled and burned the guardhouse because of being given spoiled bread. In the saloons of Mattoon, Illinois, the town where they were quartered, they had earned the name, "Governor Yates' Hellions."

Grant accepted Yates' appointment. On June 16, 1861, dressed in an old coat, out at the elbows, and a plug hat, he took the horsecar from Springfield to Mattoon. The young ruffians took one look at their new colonel and began baiting him with jeers and jostling. One blow knocked Grant's hat into the dirt. Quietly, he stooped down, picked it up, dusted it off and replaced it, saying not one word. Then he turned around and gave the group such a stern, unflinching look that each man there realized what it means to have a "commanding officer."

The deadline for re-enlistment was June 28. When the day arrived, Grant, equipped with a new uniform and a horse, faced his troops. In 10 days, the ragamuffin farm boys had become a disciplined corps. Morale had so improved that almost every man there signed the three-year enlistment papers. The regiment's first march was to Quincy, Illinois, on the Mississippi River. From there, the troops were ordered to Cairo, Illinois, where the Ohio River flowed into the Mississippi. It was a strategic place for Grant to begin his command.

Although railroads were starting to take traffic from waterways, the great Mississippi River was still the major artery which carried goods to and from the nation's heartland. Also, its valleys were the entryways to the West. Besides, railroads could be blown up; rivers could not. Obviously, whichever side controlled the Mississippi would win the war.

GENERAL GRANT

Before proceeding to Cairo, Grant received news that would help him in his rise to new acclaim. Realizing the need for more top officers, President Lincoln had asked Union congressmen for recommendations. Grant's congressman, Elihu Washburne, submitted Grant's name. On August 7, 1861, Grant received word that he had been commissioned a brigadier general, one of 36 appointed at that time.,

Before leaving for Cairo, Grant offered John Rawlins, his friend from Galena, a position of captain on his staff. Rawlins proved to be such a trusted and valuable man that he remained with Grant for the rest of his life. Eventually, Rawlins rose to the rank of brigadier general. Then, when Grant became General of the Army, Rawlins became his chief-of-staff, a position that Grant created especially for Rawlins.

To Grant, Rawlins' greatest asset was his ability to be firm and say, "No." Much of Grant's precious time and energy were conserved because of Rawlins' decisiveness.

At Cairo, Grant came under the command of General John C. Fremont, who had been the Republican candidate for President in 1856. Though in charge of the Missouri area, Fremont was a man of limited practical military ability. He did, however, recognize the strategic importance of the Mississippi River. If he made no other intelligent decision during the war, Fremont's placement of Ulysses Grant in charge at Cairo was a brilliant move. It gave Grant control of southern Illinois and southeastern Missouri. Having spent his youth travelling to the boat landings along the Mississippi and its tributaries, and chatting with steamboat crews, Grant knew the river and its quirks.

The day after Grant took command at Cairo, a scout arrived from General Fremont's headquarters. He reported that Confederate troops were headed for Paducah, Kentucky, located at the mouth of the Tennessee River, a gateway to the South. Clearly, if the North wanted to control the Mississippi, it had to get to Paducah before the Confederates. Moreover, Kentucky, which had been trying to maintain its neutrality in the war, was being wooed by both the North and the South.

Grant Secures Kentucky for the Union

Rather than wait for orders from Fremont, which might delay him, Grant telegraphed the general that he was proceeding to Paducah unless he heard otherwise. At that time, Cairo was a naval base, and three gunboats were lying at anchor there. Quickly, Grant ordered the boats manned, and embarked with two regiments. Under cover of night, the boats steamed eastward 45 miles to Paducah. They arrived at dawn, September 6, 1861, surprising the local inhabitants. The city was captured without a single shot being fired. Grant's prompt

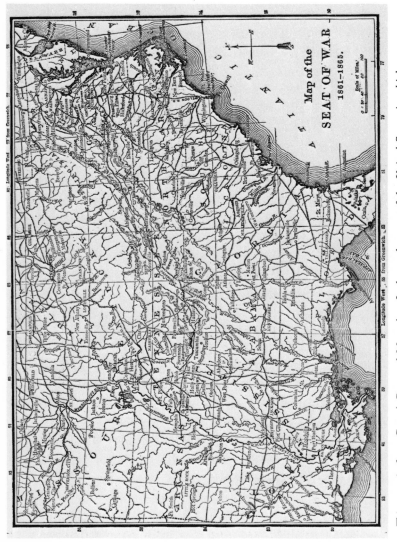

This map is from Grant's Personal Memoirs. It shows the part of the United States in which most of the major Civil War battles were fought. (Library of Congress.)

action had stopped the enemy and kept Kentucky from being overrun by the South.

With men now stationed at Paducah, Grant controlled the mouth of both the Cumberland and Tennessee Rivers. He spent the fall of 1861 consolidating his command of 20,000 soldiers and preparing for his next move.

With the help of Commodore Andrew Foote, whom he had met in Cairo, Grant was also learning the possibilities of naval warfare. Foote was a crusty character who, like Grant, believed in making decisions and taking action. Both men felt that the next step should be the capture of Fort Henry on the Tennessee and Fort Donelson on the Cumberland. Both forts were under the command of a very able Confederate general, Albert S. Johnston. With these two forts in Union hands, the way would be open to Nashville and Chattanooga, two important cities in Tennessee.

GRANT AND HIS MEN UNDER FIRE

The victory at Paducah had satisfied the government, but Grant's men had not yet been tested in battle. By November 1861, both the troops and Grant were eager for action. South of his headquarters at Cairo was the Confederate-held town of Belmont, Missouri. Grant, in an exploratory move, shipped five regiments downstream. Though he did not intend anything of the kind when he started out from Cairo, in his autobiography Grant explains, "I saw that the officers and men were elated at the prospect of at last having the opportunity of doing what they had volunteered to do—fight the enemy. I did not see how I could maintain discipline or retain confidence of my command if we should return to Cairo without any effort to do something."

Though the troops were initially successful, they were finally routed by the Confederate forces. Despite the defeat, however, Grant's men gained confidence in their command-ing officer and in their own ability under fire.

Handling Dishonest War Contractors

As 1862 approached, Grant was faced with two problems. As a former quartermaster now working hard to organize his command and ready it for action, he had no patience with shady businessmen who tried to profit from the war. Con-tractors who wished to do business with the government were supposed to submit sealed bids so that the purchasing agent could buy at the lowest price. In reality, many contractors would get together and agree to set their own prices, and the government often ended up paying exorbitant prices for such items as clothing, grain, and forage. When Grant realized what was happening, he immediately cancelled such contracts.

It did not take long for a prominent Republican politi-cian, Leonard Swett, to call upon Grant. Swett explained that he represented several very unhappy businessmen. If Grant did not stop interfering in their deals, Swett would see that Grant was relieved of his command. Furious, Grant told Swett he would continue to buy when and where he got the best price. "And," he added, "if you ever enter my military district, I shall have you imprisoned—or better yet, I'll have you shot!"

Swett did go to President Lincoln and relate what had occurred at Grant's headquarters. Lincoln listened patiently and wryly responded, "If I were you, Swett, I'd stay away from Grant. If Grant threatened to shoot you, he's just the kind of man to go ahead and do it."

Grant continued to have a free hand in ordering supplies.

VICTORY AND ANOTHER NEW NAME

Grant was not as fortunate in having a free hand with the plans that he and Commodore Foote had devised for capturing Fort

Henry and Fort Donelson. Fremont had been replaced by General Henry Wager Halleck, known to West Pointers as "Old Brains" because he had written several military texts. Command of the Western Front along the Mississippi was also shared with General George B. McClellan and General Don Carlos Buell. Each of the three had ambitions to become supreme commander.

Impatient for action, Grant approached Halleck early in January 1862, outlining an attack on Fort Henry. Halleck called the plan preposterous and, after 10 minutes, sent Grant back to Cairo. But Grant was persistent. Later that month, in separate wires, Grant and Foote both urged adoption of the plan to take Fort Henry before additional Confederate troops could reach it. This time, Halleck gave his approval. Within 24 hours, 15,000 men were on transports under the protection of seven of Foote's gunboats. Arriving at Fort Henry, they found the place half under water due to flood conditions. Before all of Grant's men reached their positions and before the Confederates could mobilize, Foote ordered his gunboats to begin bombarding the fort. Within an hour and a half, the Confederates surrendered to Commodore Foote. It was agreed between the two friends that Grant would have the pleasure of notifying Halleck of the successful opera-tion. Included in the message was the news that Foote and Grant were now on their way to capture Fort Donelson.

For a month, Buell, McClellan, and Halleck had been planning an offensive against Johnston's forces, but they could not come to any agreement as to which one of them should do so. Since Grant was under Halleck's command, Grant's success at Fort Henry now gave Halleck the edge. He promptly ordered reinforcements for Grant.

It took but 10 days, from the capture of Fort Henry on February 6, to the surrender of Fort Donelson on February 16. But it was a hard-fought victory because Grant's men were outnumbered. During the first few days, Foote's new iron-clad vessels were severely damaged and he himself was wounded. While checking on the injured naval officer, Grant learned that the Confederates had launched an attack. Grabbing a cigar that Foote offered him, Grant stuck it in his mouth, unlit, and raced back to his men. He found them without ammunition and beginning to retreat. Several soldiers stopped him to report that Confederate troops had enough rations in their knapsacks to last for three days. They were sure this meant that the enemy was preparing for a long fight. Grant interpreted the information differently. He told the men, "Only soldiers preparing to escape would carry provisions for several days."

Quickly, Grant ordered ammunition brought to the front. Riding up and down the lines, he called out, "The enemy is trying to escape and he must not be permitted to do so!" Grant's words took immediate effect. The men had only been waiting for orders.

Grant ordered his generals on both the right and left flanks to attack. By nightfall, his troops were camped well within the original Confederate lines. By early morning, a white flag fluttered over the fort. The Confederate general, Simon Buckner, the same man who had loaned Grant money to pay a hotel bill, asked for a meeting to discuss terms of surrender. Despite his admiration for Buckner, Grant sent back the following reply: "No terms except an unconditional and immediate surrender can be accepted." Buckner had no choice but to accept Grant's terms.

"Unconditional Surrender" Grant

The effect of Grant's words echoed and re-echoed throughout the North. Now the newspapers began to play up Grant's every word and action. The story about his galloping back to his men with a cigar stuck in his mouth resulted in many boxes of cigars being sent to Grant's headquarters. (In reality, Grant had been a pipe-smoker, and those who remembered him from earlier days recall his walking about with a pipe between his teeth. It was because of the many gifts that Grant switched from a pipe to cigars.)

The North needed a real victory for its sagging morale. Here it was: a successful two-day battle involving both military and naval forces. The cost in casualties had been great on both sides, but never before had so many prisoners been taken in battle on this continent. The capture of Fort Donelson gave Kentucky to the North and forced Johnston to pull his forces back to the state of Mississippi.

Halleck was pleased with Grant's success. He telegraphed the news to Washington in hopes that Lincoln would now commission him, Halleck, to be supreme commander of the West. But Lincoln, having carefully reviewed the reports, recommended only one promotion for the Senate's approval—that of U.S. Grant to the rank of major general. It was promptly confirmed.

Overnight, Grant became a national hero. People who had never heard of the casually attired little general from Galena discovered that U.S. Grant really meant "Unconditional Surrender" Grant.

Halleck bitterly resented the publicity and the pictures of Grant that appeared on the front pages of the northern newspapers. In communications to the President and to General McClellan, he took every opportunity to complain about Grant's reports or lack of them. (It was later learned that some of Grant's telegrams had never been received due to a mix-up in the telegraph center.) Finally, Halleck relieved Grant of his command and sent him back to Fort Henry.

Grant was on the verge of resigning when Halleck was appointed supreme commander of the West. With the prize in his hands, Halleck was in a more generous mood. He also needed Grant for the coming campaign. In an attempt to smooth matters over, Halleck sent Grant a letter in which he said, "Instead of relieving you, I wish you, as soon as your new army is in the field, to assume immediate command and lead it to new victories."

In spite of his personal feelings, Grant knew where his duty lay. He proceeded southward on the Tennessee River to join his troops.

Chapter 4

Vicksburg and Vindication

Battles and even wars can be won or lost by prompt decisions or a missed opportunity. Grant always believed that the war could have ended sooner had the victory at Fort Donelson been followed up immediately by a forward advance on the Confederate forces. The morale of the Confederates was low and it was hard for them to find fresh recruits. The time to attack was now—before the Confederates had a chance to regroup their forces. But a whole month of niggling negotiations between Halleck and McClellan gave the shattered Confederate army time to reconcentrate their troops at a vital railroad junction, the town of Corinth, Mississippi.

Now top commander of the Western Front, Halleck ordered Grant and Buell to bring their forces to Shiloh, a point on the Tennessee River that was 25 miles north of Corinth. Here, Grant had stationed General William T. Sherman, an early supporter of Grant who had offered his services on several occasions. An enduring bond would grow between these two men. From Shiloh, the massed Union forces would march on Corinth.

What the Union generals had not counted on was that Johnston would decide to take aggressive action rather than wait patiently for the enemy. Buell had not yet arrived and the Union troops had not yet built trenches. (It was thought at the time that digging ditches lowered morale.) Confederate soldiers had been sighted in the woods, but they were assumed to be advancing scouts. The Union forces were totally unprepared for what was about to happen.

TRAGEDY AT SHILOH

At dawn, April 6, 1862, 40,000 Confederate troops attacked 33,000 unsuspecting Yankees in three successive waves. All day long, the Confederates pounded away. Time after time, they seemed on the verge of victory. Each time, they were repulsed.

When Grant arrived from his headquarters upriver, he quickly moved from one part of the field to another, encouraging the men, giving orders to the officers. By evening, Buell and his troops had arrived, as had another 5,000 men led by General Lew Wallace. All night long, Union gunboats shelled the Confederate lines. A heavy downpour soaked the battlefield and added to the misery of the men.

Some time after midnight, Grant sought shelter and rest in a loghouse that had been converted into a field hospital. He watched the suffering of the wounded, the amputation of a leg or an arm, until he could no longer bear the sights and sounds. Sherman found him later, sitting in the rain, leaning against a tree, hat pulled down and coat collar pulled up.

The fighting was just as fierce the second day, but this time, aided by the fresh troops of Buell and Wallace, the Union forces drove the Confederates back. By three o'clock in the afternoon, General Pierre Beauregard, one of the Confederate leaders, had no choice but to order a retreat. Union troops, too weary to pursue the enemy, settled back into their camps to tend to their wounds and count their losses.

The battle of Shiloh was one of the bloodiest in history.

It was not battle between two professional armies. The troops on both sides were volunteers: young lads from farms; raw, young immigrants from coastal cities; educated young men from the "best families," hoping to rise through the officer ranks. Some sought excitement; some felt the fervor of patriotism flourishing throughout the land. Most of these young men had never held a musket, nor had many of them ever seen a battlefield. Some fled within the first half hour after the battle began and cowered, paralyzed with fear, at the river banks. Yet most of them, the very best that the North and the South had to offer, proved themselves men of stamina and courage.

More than 20,000 Confederate and Union soldiers were reported dead, wounded, or missing in action. Black ribbons of mourning hung in homes throughout the North and South. There were also bitter feelings against the generals who were involved, especially Grant. In some quarters, gossip about Grant's tendency to drink (false though it was) began to spread.

LINCOLN PROCLAIMS FREEDOM FOR SLAVES

From April to January of 1863, the Army of the West moved slowly southward. In September, Grant's men captured Corinth, reviving his reputation as a capable commander. On September 22, 1863, President Lincoln announced the Emancipation Proclamation. Because it freed all slaves in the Confederate states, the proclamation made it possible for Union generals fighting in these areas to accept fugitive slaves into their camps. Previously, slaves had been turned away or civilian slave-holders were allowed to come into some of the camps to seek out their "property." Grant was ahead of his time; he had never permitted his soldiers to do either.

Grant's View of the War

At the beginning of the war, Grant, like many others, viewed it as necessary to preserve the Union. His actions clearly revealed his antislavery feelings, but he had never taken a public stand on the issue. Yet, in a plodding, thoughtful manner, Grant's ideas had slowly been evolving. In letters to his family, even before the Emancipation Proclamation, he saw himself as serving in an Army of Liberation. "It would take a standing army to maintain slavery in the South if we were to make peace today. . . . The North and South [can] never live at peace with each other except as one nation and that without slavery."

When the proclamation came, Grant was ready. He had already discovered that fugitive slaves made excellent guides. For armies marching in unfamiliar areas, fugitive blacks offered helpful advice. Maps could never detail the kind of information and advice that local blacks could. Moreover, many of them saved the army money and manpower by taking over such jobs as teamsters, cooks, and laborers.

Now, with the proclamation, the trickle of fugitive slaves became a flood. New preparations had to be made to handle the large numbers of refugees appearing in army camps. Grant had an idea for using slaves that was probably the beginning of what would later be called the "Freedman's Bureau."

A Plan for the Freedman

Armies cannot move easily when encumbered by large numbers of refugees in need of food and work. As the Union armies approached, many local southerners fled, leaving deserted plantations with ripening corn and cotton that needed to be harvested. Grant's idea was to employ men, women, and children above the age of 10 to do this work. In this way, crops could be saved and the monies received used to house and feed the workers. What was needed was a compassionate man with imagination and good organizational skills to run the operation. The man Grant selected was John Eaton, a chaplain from New Hampshire. Eaton was a graduate of Dartmouth College and, before the war, had been Superintendent of Schools in Toledo, Ohio.

Grant was in the midst of preparing what was to be his longest and most daring military campaign. Yet, in his meeting with Eaton, Grant took considerable time to explain his own ideas on slavery and offer practical suggestions on how the project might be started. Eaton at first expressed reservations about the plan and personal concerns about leaving his work as chaplain. But Grant was quietly persuasive. "The camp at Grand Junction has thousands of slaves in need of help," he explained. "As our armies arrived, the local residents fled. They were kind enough to leave behind deserted houses and empty buildings. I know the Negro is going to prove himself as a free and independent worker. We need to begin here and now to give him that opportunity." Eaton listened to Grant. There was no question about both the passion and the practicality of the man's words.

Eaton turned out to be a capable and efficient organizer. Grant promised him men and supplies for his work, and he kept his word. There were those soldiers who were reluctant to work alongside the newly freed slaves, but under Grant's directives, they cooperated. In time, much more than food, shelter, and work were provided. People from the North began to offer assistance in educating the former slaves and in giving them medical and other services. The road to real freedom would be a long one, but those travelling it were off to a good start with Eaton and Grant. After the war, Eaton served for many years as the United States Commissioner of Education.

Blacks Fight in the Civil War

At the beginning of the Civil War, when northern blacks tried to enlist as soldiers in the Union army, their offers to serve were rejected. In spite of the fact that blacks were currently serving in the navy and had previously fought in the Revolutionary War and the War of 1812, many northerners believed strongly that the Civil War was a "white man's war." Some objected to fighting alongside blacks; others questioned the black man's courage in the heat of battle.

But Frederick Douglas, the great black leader, argued, "Once let a black man get upon his person the brass letters, U.S., let him get an eagle on his button, and a musket on his shoulder and bullets in his pocket, and there is no power on earth which can deny that he has earned the right to citizenship in the United States."

Blacks were already serving as scouts, teamsters, carpenters, blacksmiths . . . and spies. Allan Pinkerton, chief of the U.S. Secret Service, had found great success using blacks to get information behind enemy lines. Many captured Union soldiers owed their lives to blacks who helped them find their way through Confederate lines to freedom.

Then, in 1862, the Union army suffered a series of blows. It had been defeated in several important battles, troop morale was low, and recruits were few. In July, Congress passed laws permitting freed blacks to enlist. The first black regiments were organized in the South Carolina Sea Islands, urged by teachers and missionaries to fight for their own freedom and to prove that blacks deserved the same rights as whites. These first black regiments succeeded in capturing and occupying Jacksonville, Florida. The reports back to the secretary of war and the northern press were so glowing that black regiments were organized from Massachusetts to New Orleans.

It took considerably more courage for blacks to enlist than for whites. In May 1863, Jefferson Davis, President of the Confederate States, proclaimed that captured black officers would be put to death. There were, in fact, several reports of black soldiers who were either shot or sold into slavery. But Davis' ruling about black officers was unnecessary because there were very few of them—most black regiments were led by whites.

Blacks also had other problems. Often, black enlistees were paid less than whites. In South Carolina, blacks in the 54th and 55th regiments refused to accept any pay until they were given the same amount as whites. It took almost two years for Congress to assure equality of pay to black soldiers.

In battle after battle, black soldiers proved their courage and intelligence. Reports came to Washington from generals in the field applauding the efforts of the black regiments. Black enlistments continued despite the fact that black soldiers were on occasion beaten up by whites in the streets of northern cities.

In June 1863, black regiments proved their ability at the battle of Milliken's Bend near Vicksburg and in the battle around Petersburg, Virginia. By October 1864, there were 140 black regiments in the Union army. Almost 200,000 black men participated in every Union campaign during 1864–1865 except Sherman's march through Georgia. They not only served in the infantry, but in the artillery and the cavalry as well. By the war's end, several blacks were commissioned as lieutenants, and eight surgeons were given medical commissions carrying the rank of major.

The success of black soldiers in the North may well have influenced the decision of the Confederates to also use black troops. At first, President Davis had stubbornly refused to consider the idea. But after General Robert E. Lee urged Davis to reconsider, a law was passed in January 1865 that allowed blacks to enlist in the Confederate army. However, they would *not* be emancipated. The war ended before any such regiments could be organized.

Blacks made up almost 10 percent of the Union forces. About 37,000 of these men lost their lives. For their valor, 17 black soldiers and four black sailors earned the nation's highest military award, the Congressional Medal of Honor.

Grant Moves On

With his plan for the liberated blacks now being implemented by Eaton, Grant could focus on his plan to capture Vicksburg, Mississippi. The elections of 1862 had gone against the Republicans. Many northerners were discouraged by a war that seemed endless and inconclusive. Throughout most of the North, voluntary enlistments had dropped so low that Lincoln was forced to draft men into service.

Some generals advocated going back north to establish Memphis, Tennessee, as a supply base, then coming south again by rail. It was Grant's considered judgment that such a backward move would be a mistake. In addition, something in Grant's personality nearly always kept him from retracing his steps.

Indeed, Grant's final decision to move his armies forward would prove to be one of the most important decisions of the Civil War.

THE STRATEGY AT VICKSBURG

The prize was Vicksburg, Mississippi, a city built on a high bluff at the tip of a horseshoe bend in the Mississippi River, about 200 miles south of Memphis. Vicksburg was an important railroad center. One rail line extended from the west bank of the Mississippi River westward to Shreveport, Louisiana. Another rail line from Vicksburg ran through the South. Vicksburg was the only link between the parts of the Confederacy divided by the Mississippi River. As long as Vicksburg was held by the Confederacy, their troops, supplies, and goods for market could be transported eastward. Moreover, free navigation of the river by the North was not possible. If Vicksburg could be captured, however, the South would be split in two and the road opened for conquest of the Confederacy.

But attacking Vicksburg would require some imaginative strategies. The area surrounding the city was a tangle of bayous and creeks. One of Grant's ideas was to short-circuit the Mississippi by digging a canal through the thin neck of land opposite Vicksburg. Such a canal would change the course of the river and drain the area around Vicksburg. Union ships and men could then bypass the horseshoe bend and attack Vicksburg from the south.

Another scheme was to attack from the North, but General John Pemberton, the commander of the Confederate forces at Vicksburg, anticipated this plan. A third strategy was for Grant's forces to move south on the west side of the river until they reached a point 20 miles or more below Vicksburg. If Union gunboats and transports could navigate safely past the Confederate guns at Vicksburg and pick up the Union forces waiting south of the city, they could then ferry them to the east bank and attack the Confederates from the rear. But all Grant's plans required waiting for awhile, when the roads would not be muddy and troop movements could be swift.

Confusing the Enemy

During the long winter of 1862–1863, 4,000 of Grant's men labored in vain digging the canal, which, in March, was destroyed by a flood. Realizing the canal was not the answer, Grant nevertheless kept his men busy seeking other routes through the bayous. One reason was to toughen his soldiers for what lay ahead; another was to mislead Pemberton.

Indeed, Pemberton had good reason to be confused. Earlier, General William Sherman had been deployed to Chickasaw Bluffs, north of Vicksburg. He attempted to seize the town, but Pemberton, in a bloody engagement, repulsed the attack. But because Sherman's troops were still in the area north of Vicksburg, it seemed obvious to Pemberton that the

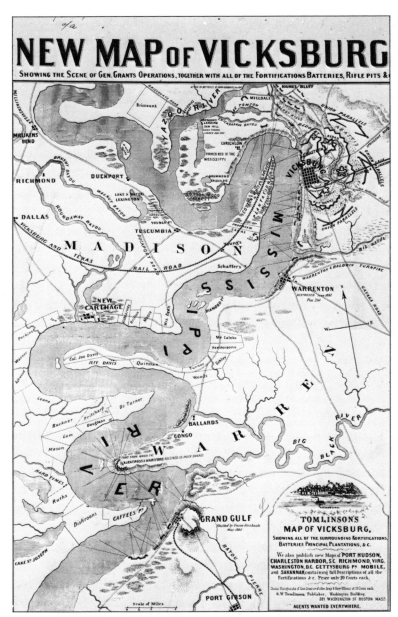

A map showing the battlefields and surrounding areas of
Vicksburg. (Library of Congress.)

Union forces would be coming through the bayous from the north.

The Navy Helps

On April 16, 1863, Grant made his first move. Under the cover of darkness, Union gunboats and transports slipped downstream and then sped past the booming cannons at Vicksburg. Despite the Confederate bombardment, only one ship was sunk.

Next, Grant began moving his troops south along the west bank of the river, out of sight of the Confederate forces. To divert Pemberton's attention, Sherman also began moving, as if going back to Chickasaw Bluffs. The tactic worked. Too late, Pemberton realized that Grant's army of more than 40,000 men had marched south and had been ferried across the river, apparently poised to strike at Vicksburg from the south.

Grant's next move further confused Pemberton. Grant knew that the very capable Confederate general, Joseph Johnston, was in Jackson, Mississippi, the state capital, and that Johnston's army must be defeated before it could send support to General Pemberton. So, instead of marching north, Grant's men, with five days of rations in their packs, began marching east to Jackson. Once again, the men lived off the land, filling farm wagons with food from the storerooms or smokehouses of plantations along the way. Before other Confederate troops could arrive to support Johnston's men, Jackson was in Union hands.

Fred Grant, the general's oldest son and a lad still in his teens, had accompanied his father throughout the campaign. As soon as the guns at Jackson became silent, Fred and a newspaper reporter, Sylvanus Cadwallader, dashed to the capitol building to lower the Confederate flag. They had almost reached the roof when they came face to face with a muddy Union cavalryman, the flag clutched to his chest. Reluctantly, Fred accepted the fact someone else would deliver the prize to his father.

THE CAPTURE OF VICKSBURG

Meanwhile, Grant was preoccupied with a bigger prize — Vicksburg. Johnston's army was in disarray. Sherman had destroyed Jackson as a southern railroad and manufacturing center. (At one factory, the women workers and their manager seemed unaware that Grant and Sherman had entered the building. Both men were amazed. Finally, Grant gave orders for the workers to stop what they were doing, take as many cotton bolts as they could carry, and then leave. A few moments later, the factory was ablaze.) Grant was now ready to move on to Vicksburg.

By May 19th, Pemberton's forces were driven back into Vicksburg, and Union trenches encircled the area. But it was not until July 4, 1863, that the siege of Vicksburg ended and Pemberton surrendered.

By a strange coincidence, it was on that same Independence Day of 1863 that the battle of Gettysburg ended. The Confederate attempt to push the war into Union territory in the hills of Pennsylvania had failed. With victories in both the west and the east and with the Mississippi River now controlled by the Union, a new spirit of optimism spread through the North. Lincoln sent Grant a letter of congratulations and later promoted him to supreme commander in the West.

However, what Grant really wanted was the opportunity to move on. By striking again, while the Confederacy was still reeling from the loss of Vicksburg, Grant believed he could successfully penetrate the heart of the South and destroy its food supplies and munition plants. But General Halleck, his superior, would not hear of it. For one thing,

Halleck was angry that Grant had paroled more than 30,000 weary Confederate soldiers. (Grant, however, reasoned that these war-sickened men would rather return home than fight; thus, to release them would save both the time and the money needed to transport them to prisons in the north.) More important, Hallack, always cautious, wanted to secure the newly won territory with garrisons scattered throughout the area.

THE BATTLE OF CHATTANOOGA

After their many victories, Union troops then suffered a serious defeat at Chickamauga, Tennessee, and had to fall back to Chattanooga, a major railroad center and a gateway to the Deep South. Surrounded in Chattanooga, the Union forces were now in the same state of seige as the Confederate troops had been at Vicksburg. The confederates held two key positions on the high ground overlooking the city—Lookout Mountain and Missionary Ridge—and as long as they controlled these positions, the Union general at Chattanooga, William Rosecrans, could not get food and other supplies. Men and horses were slowly starving within the city.

"Get Grant!"

President Lincoln and Secretary of War Edwin Stanton were of one mind: "Get Grant!" Telegraph wires burned with frantic messages to Grant, who had gone to New Orleans to check the situation there.

Unfortunately, while Grant was reviewing troops in New Orleans, the expert horseman suffered a terrible accident. The noise from a passing steam engine had caused his very spirited horse to rear and fall atop Grant, who was knocked unconscious and had to endure weeks of excruciating pain from a swollen leg. The telegrams from Washington arrived while he was still recovering from the accident.

By the end of October, however, Grant managed to get to Chattanooga. Sometimes he used crutches and needed help getting on his horse. Other times, he had to be carried on a litter. Nevertheless, on the day of his arrival, he immediately sat down with the generals to assess the situation and to make plans. Within a few days, the morale of the half-starved troops began to improve as supply lines were reopened and food rations were given to the men. Their confidence was restored as Grant began to pull the operation together.

Victory at Chattanooga

At last, Lady Luck was riding with Grant! General Braxton Bragg, the commander in chief of the Confederate forces, and his generals at Chattanooga had been unable to agree on a plan of action. When Bragg sent General James Longstreet's troops to a location 100 miles away, thereby reducing the Confederate strength, Grant seized the opportunity to attack the Confederate positions at three points on the mountain slopes around Chattanooga.

On November 25th, three Union armies under Generals Joseph Hooker, William T. Sherman, and George Thomas took their assigned positions. At about four o'clock in the afternoon, six cannons were fired, one right after another. Suddenly, with bugles blaring attack signals and the cries of officers urging their men forward, Union forces attacked the Confederate positions from three sides.

During this battle, one of the greatest—and most unexpected—events in military history occurred. The soldiers assigned to attack Missionary Ridge had been ordered to take only the first line of Confederate trenches and then wait for the rest of the army to reform for the next assault. But these troops were experienced veterans. When they saw the Confederates in retreat, they ignored their orders and pursued the enemy to the second line of trenches.

Some reports of the battle state that Grant was furious at this lack of respect for his orders. Other reports say that he actually encouraged the men to press on. Whatever his attitude, there is no doubt that the results played into his hands. Instead of stopping, the Union forces continued to pursue the Confederate troops while crying, "Take the ridge! Take the ridge!"

When one of the Union generals reached the top of the ridge, he shouted to his cheering soldiers, "You'll all be court-martialed," at which they all burst into laughter.

SUPREME COMMANDER OF THE UNION ARMY

The victory at Chattanooga was one of the most dramatic of the war. The country began to realize that Ulysses Grant's plans and decisive actions had produced more important victories than any other Union general.

There was no doubt now in Lincoln's mind about what the nation needed most. Too much time and too many lives had been lost by generals who lacked vision and could not move quickly. In March 1864, Lincoln called Grant to Washington and appointed him supreme commander of the Union army.

Chapter 5

Appomattox and Assassination

U lysses Grant's arrival in Washington had the same comic air as his arrival at West Point 25 years earlier. Who would haved suspected that the short, stooped man in the seedy-looking general's uniform, clutching the hand of his 14-year-old son, was the hero of the hour? Certainly not the desk clerk at the Willard Hotel. He looked blankly at the weary man who signed the register and, without even reading the name, handed him a key to a small room on the fifth floor. As Grant and young Fred started across the lobby, people began to surround the pair. The clerk now hurriedly checked the register, where he saw the entry, "Ulysses S. Grant and son, Galena, Illinois." Within minutes, Ulysses and Fred were ushered ceremoniously to the suite of rooms that had been ordered earlier for them by the War Department.

For a man who was quite shy and had modest expectations, Grant found the furor of Washington politics and society more than a little overwhelming. But from a personal standpoint, his trip there was very rewarding indeed.

While accompanying his father through the Vicksburg campaign, Fred had become seriously ill. Later, when Fred was in St. Louis during the Chattanooga campaign, Grant received word that his son might be dying and rushed to St. Louis to be at his side. Fred's recovery and the opportunity to take his son to meet the President in the White House gave extra-special importance to their visit to Washington.

GRANT MEETS LINCOLN

On the evening of his arrival, Grant, unannounced, attended a gathering at the White House. President Lincoln, his tall figure towering above the crowd, noticed him come in.

"General Grant," announced the President. "So pleased to meet you."

Grant was barely able to exchange greetings with the President and Mrs. Lincoln when people began to mill around, pushing and shoving to get a better look at the hero of Chattanooga. To add to Grant's embarrassment, Secretary of State William Seward persuaded the general to stand up on a sofa so everyone could see him.

No wonder Grant was more than anxious to retreat to his new headquarters with the Army of the Potomac. For two months, after studying all aspects of the war, he drew several important conclusions. One was that the reason the war had lasted so long was because the Union generals had not coordinated their efforts. Two Confederate armies had to be defeated. One was the Army of Northern Virginia, led by Robert E. Lee, the most famous of all Confederate generals. The other was the Army of the Tennessee, led by Joseph Johnston, another southern general whom Grant respected. Under his unified command, Grant made these two Confederate armies his most important military targets.

Another conclusion was that the war would not end until the economy of the South had been smashed. Railroads, supply lines, and cash crops that might help the southern cause had to be destroyed.

The final conclusion was that three years of fighting in the eastern states had brought few victories to the North. Lee, in fact, had managed to push the Army of the Potomac northward in one humiliating defeat after another. The Union troops were experienced veterans. They knew how to fight. Now they had to learn how to win!

As the supreme commander, Grant was both courteous and kind to those under whom he had served. He also knew the strengths and the weaknesses of the generals now serving him. With the command now unified under his direction, Grant began to deploy his armies.

THE BEGINNING OF THE END

In May 1864, General Sherman, starting from Chattanooga, began to march to Atlanta, Georgia. At the same time, Grant, determined not to be an "armchair general," accompanied General George C. Meade and the Army of the Potomac to the Confederate capital at Richmond, Virginia. Their first battle took place in rough and tangled woods called "The Wilderness." The rifle fire was so intense that the trees caught fire, and both sides lost many men in the blazing inferno. The North alone suffered more than 17,000 casualties.

Although people were appalled at the number of deaths at The Wilderness, Grant continued to march south toward Richmond. The Army of the Potomac was learning that, with Grant in charge, there was no turning back.

Because the North would not tolerate another battle in which so many men were killed, Grant had a plan for capturing Richmond that he hoped would minimize the number of casualties. Rather than an overland frontal attack, which the Union had tried unsuccessfully for three years, Grant would go around Richmond, cross the James River on pontoon bridges, and attack the city from the south. The operation was much like the strategy used at Vicksburg. It worked so well that three days passed before Lee discovered Grant's forces were no longer in The Wilderness.

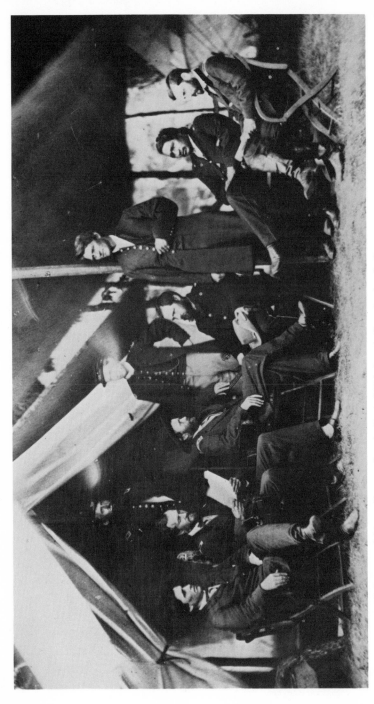

This photograph of Grant and his staff was taken in June 1864, just before the battle for Petersburg, Virginia. Seated from left to right are Colonel John Rawlins, Colonel C.B. Comstock, General Grant, Major M.M. Morgan, Colonel Ely S. Parker, and Colonel O.E. Babcock. (Library of Congress.)

Atlanta and Petersburg Fall

Grant now moved toward Petersburg, a town where three railroad lines met, only 20 miles south of Richmond. Among the troops who attacked Petersburg in June were four regiments of black volunteers. Under heavy artillery fire, the soldiers succeeded in capturing part of the fortification. Unfortunately, other regiments were not as successful and the siege of Petersburg was to continue for many more months.

During the rest of the summer and the fall of 1864, Grant's men used picks and shovels to destroy the railroad that ran into Richmond. Meanwhile, Sherman was meeting with far more success than Grant. On September 2, Atlanta fell to Sherman and the city was put to the torch. This victory was followed by General Philip Sheridan's march through the Shenandoah Valley of Virginia. Food, forage, and cattle were either taken or destroyed. With these victories to report to the nation, Lincoln's re-election in November was assured.

However, the campaign in Virginia was far from over. But Grant had a plan: he would engage Lee in a series of exhausting battles in the trenches around Petersburg and thus prevent Lee from joining forces with Johnston's Army of the Tennessee. Nor would Lee be able to aid any other southern troops. The strategy worked.

On April 3, 1865, Grant's armies captured both Petersburg and Richmond. Lee made one last attempt to break through to the south to join Johnston, but Grant cut off his last avenue of escape. With no food and half of his soldiers too weak to hold a weapon, Lee was forced to surrender.

LEE SURRENDERS AT APPOMATTOX

On April 9th, Lee and Grant met in the house of a Mr. McLean in Appomattox, Virginia. Grant arrived wearing a

The Indian at Appomattox

When General Robert E. Lee signed the terms of surrender at Appomattox, standing near Grant was his trusted secretary, a full-blooded Seneca Indian, General Ely S. Parker. The friendship between Grant and Parker developed during Grant's Galena days, when Parker was sent to Galena to supervise the construction of a customs house for the United States Army.

Parker was born on the Seneca reservation in Genesee County, New York, the son of a Seneca chieftain and an Iroquois mother, the daughter of a chief. He was given an Indian name meaning ''The Wolf.'' His first job was caring for horses at a Canadian military post, where white boys would bait him and make his life miserable. Though in line to become a chief, Parker decided to outdo his tormentors by getting an education, first at a missionary school and later at two nearby private academies. He went on to study law but discovered that he could not practice in the state of New York. As an Indian, he was not a United States citizen. He then began studying at Rensselaer Polytechnic Institute in Troy, New York, and became a civil engineer. It was this work which brought him to Galena in 1857.

Though living outside the reservation, Parker did not abandon his people. When Indians petitioned the government for permission to keep their lands, the handsome and quick-witted young Parker accompanied lawyers and chiefs on their trips to Washington to help the Indians argue their case. It was while seeking such rights for his fellow Indians that Parker met such noted men as Daniel Webster and Henry Clay, and even dined at the White House with President Polk.

In 1852, in honor of his efforts on their behalf, Parker's tribe elected him Sachem, or chief. They gave him the name *Do-ne-ho-geh-weh*—"Keeper of the Western Door of the Long House of the Iroquois."

When the Civil War broke out, Parker returned to New York to get his father's reluctant approval to enlist. Confidently, Parker went to Washington to see Secretary of State William Henry Seward about getting a commission. Seward supposedly told him that the war "was an affair between white men and one in which the Indian was not called to act." However, this did not deter Parker. In 1863, he was appointed a captain of volunteers and joined Grant's staff for the Vicksburg campaign. He soon became attached to Grant's personal staff and accompanied him to Washington.

In 1869, in his inaugural speech, Grant called for education and citizenship for the Indians. Parker, who was Grant's model of what education could do to enable the Indian to fit into American culture, was appointed Commissioner of Indian Affairs. To implement the new government policies toward Indians, Quakers, noted for their gentle ways and concern for others, were assigned to several reservations to replace the businessmen called Indian agents.

Grant and Parker were not to realize their hopes for the Indians, but had their plans worked, they might have proved a milestone in Indian affairs.

Ely Parker's friendship endured through Grant's presidency and beyond. One of the men permitted to visit with Grant during his last tragic illness was his old friend, General Ely Parker.

soldier's blouse for a coat and only tarnished shoulder straps showing his rank. His boots and his trousers were spattered with mud.

Lee arrived attired in an immaculate gray uniform. He wore embroidered gloves, and his dress sword swung at his side. There was little expression on the face of the elegant and dignified Lee. Looking up at the six-foot man before him, a sense of sadness and depression overcame Grant. "I felt like anything rather than rejoicing at the downfall of a foe who had fought so long and valiantly." Without a doubt, anyone witnessing the scene would have found it hard to tell who was the victor and who was the vanquished.

Grant's surrender terms were among the most generous in history: the defeated soldiers would simply lay down their arms and then go home. Grant also realized that most of the soldiers were small farmers who would need horses or mules to work their farms. He therefore directed that "every man of the Confederate Army who claimed to own a horse or mule take the animal to his home." When he read this, Lee, for

This is an artist's version of the scene in the McLean House when Lee surrendered at Appomattox. Seated in the middle are General Robert E. Lee (left) and General Ulysses S. Grant, who appears to be better dressed than first-hand accounts of the event would have us believe. Standing third from the right is Colonel Ely S. Parker, Grant's aide, who acted as secretary at the proceedings. (Library of Congress.)

the first time, showed his feelings. "This will have a happy effect on my army."

Grant's own feelings about the day were summed up in his memoirs. "When news of the surrender first reached our lines, our men commenced firing a salute of a hundred guns in honor of the victory. I at once sent word, however, to have it stopped. The Confederates were now our prisoners, and we did not want to exult over their downfall."

JULIA REFUSES AN INVITATION

Julia Dent Grant was a strong-minded, capable woman. Many times during the war she had risked her life to join Ulysses at command headquarters. Many fellow officers knew how often Julia's presence had helped Grant to maintain the air of calm and self-assurance that he showed to the outside world. So it was not surprising that Grant listened to Julia's arguments about accepting a social invitation from President Lincoln.

"I do not want to go to the Ford Theater this evening," she explained. "Mrs. Lincoln made me very uncomfortable when she came to army headquarters with the President, and I will not enjoy sitting with her in the presidential box. Besides, we promised the children we would be seeing them at their school in New Jersey this weekend." Grant, the loving husband and doting father, was easy to convince. Besides, he held no great affection for the theater.

It was just five days after the surrender at Appomattox, and Grant had gone to Washington for a cabinet meeting. In the discussion that took place that day, Grant supported Lincoln's hopes that the North would be lenient in its treatment of the Confederate states. It was to be Lincoln's last meeting.

That night, at the Ford Theater in Washington, Lincoln was fatally shot. There is now little doubt that Grant would also have been a target for assassination. That evening, on the way to the railroad station for their trip to New Jersey, a horseman had followed the Grants' carriage and attempted to peer inside. Later, on the train, another man tried to force his way into their car.

Grant received the news of Lincoln's assassination that night by telegram, while waiting in Philadelphia for the ferry to New Jersey. Folding the telegram and placing it in his pocket, he turned to Julia. "This is the darkest day of my life," he said.

PRESIDENT JOHNSON TAKES OVER

Grant immediately returned to Washington. As soon as word of Lincoln's death was received, Andrew Johnson was sworn in as President. (By a strange coincidence, just about a century later, another Johnson, Lyndon Johnson, would be sworn in immediately after the assassination of President John F. Kennedy.)

The date was April 15, 1865. Within three days, the first government crisis took place. Generals William Sherman and Joseph Johnston had met in North Carolina and worked out the terms of surrender. Along with Johnston was the Confederate secretary of war, John C. Breckinridge. The treaty agreed upon was to be the official and final treaty of peace between the North and the South. All soldiers who had fought for the Confederacy would be pardoned, and the Confederate states would be readmitted to the Union.

This agreement went far beyond Grant's terms with Lee. Yet it was in keeping with the way Sherman had interpreted Lincoln's wishes when Lincoln, Grant, and Sherman had talked at army headquarters late in the war. Lincoln had summed up his position with the words, "Let 'em up easy."

But Lincoln's attitude did not reflect that of all northerners, and his assassination brought out the hatred that many of them still held for the South. Several members of Johnson's Cabinet felt that the terms of surrender were far too lenient and that Sherman had gone beyond the limits of his authority.

President Johnson and Secretary of War Stanton sent Grant to reason with Sherman. The two friends talked, and Sherman agreed to offer the Confederate general the same terms of surrender as Lee. Johnston accepted. Grant was beginning to get a taste of Washington politics.

A NATIONAL HERO

Grant was also enjoying the fruits of being the most popular man in the country. That spring, wealthy Philadelphians presented Grant with a splendid home in their city. Julia was delighted to discover that it was furnished with everything, from fine linens, beautiful silver, and a piano right down to coal for the furnace!

Once, during the war, a newspaperman asked Grant what he would do after the war. Grant, remembering the muddy road he had to slosh through when he went from his home to the leather store, answered, "I'd like to be mayor of Galena and build a sidewalk from the railroad station to my home."

That August, when Grant returned to Galena, the local townspeople were way ahead of him. As Grant got off the train, he saw a fine boardwalk stretching out before him and a big banner that read, "General, here is your sidewalk." His hometown also gave their most famous citizen a completely furnished home.

Of course, Grant's father, Jesse, was there to greet his son. Ever the businessman, he wrote an advertisement for the old store in honor of his son's visit. It read:

> Since Grant has whipped the Rebel Lee
> And opened trade from sea to sea

Our goods in price must soon advance
Then don't neglect the present chance
to call on GRANT and PERKINS
                    J.R.G.

There are no reports of Ulysses' reactions to his father's doggeral.

For several months, Grant and his family toured the North. Everywhere they went, they were greeted by parades, bands, and banquets. As grateful as Grant was for all the attention, he was always ill at ease when asked to make a speech. He'd simply mumble a few words of thanks and then sit down.

One time, when the crowds began to clamor, little Jesse turned to his father and begged him to get up and say a few words. When Grant refused, a man in the crowd shouted, "Well, if you won't speak, General, perhaps your son will!" Much to everyone's amusement, seven-year-old Jesse stood up and saved the family honor by reciting the poem, "The Boy Stood on the Burning Deck." Ulysses was both embarrassed and proud.

For Grant's family, the tour was a tiring but an exhilarating experience. It gave the people a chance to see Grant, shake his hand, and feel a part of the honors being showered upon him. For Julia and Ulysses, it was a preview of the kind of life that would be in store for them.

Not long after their tour, the Grants moved from their Philadelphia home to a new one in Washington.

Chapter 6

The Road to the Presidency

The press, politicians, and the public make our heroes and villains. Certainly, Grant's glory was promoted by all three. In the same way, Andrew Johnson, the man who succeeded Lincoln as President, was often portrayed as the villain of the postwar era. In reality, perhaps neither of these men deserved their reputations.

Like Lincoln, Johnson was a self-made, self-educated man of humble beginnings. He worked as a tailor and eventually owned a prosperous shop in Tennessee. He was a Democrat and, as a champion of the rights of the common people, hated the favored treatment given to southern plantation owners. When the Civil War broke out, Johnson was serving his first term in the Senate. Among the southern senators, he alone supported the Union. During the presidential convention in 1864, Johnson was nominated as Vice-President in order to show some southern Democratic support for the Republican platform.

POSTWAR PROBLEMS EMERGE

As Presidents during the post-Civil War era, both Grant and Johnson faced insurmountable problems. It did not help that they followed Lincoln, whose image was enhanced by the tragic way he died. Lincoln's death created a great vacuum.

For three years before he died, Lincoln had been thinking about and planning for the reunification of the states, a plan which later would be called "Reconstruction." It was to include the same kind of generosity toward the South that Grant had shown to Lee's armies. But when Lincoln died and others began to try to fill the vacuum caused by the loss of his leadership, controversial issues quickly surfaced.

The South had been devastated by the war. Civil government was gone; there were no courts, no police officers, no postal services. The port of Charleston, South Carolina, had been the pride of the South. Now it was a city of "vacant houses, widowed women, deserted warehouses, of miles of grass-grown streets and acres of pitiful barrenness."

The value of farm property and crops had dropped almost 50 percent. Manufacturing plants and railroads were destroyed. Schools were closed and, in many places, people were starving and dependent on the federal government for food.

The southern black was in a kind of no-man's land. He was no longer a slave, but neither was he really free. He had little or no education, lacked knowledge of his civil rights, and was often terrorized by bands of whites. He often went back to work for his former owner as a sharecropper or tenant farmer.

The North was also undergoing many changes of its own. As a result of the war, big profits had been made in manufacturing and railroading. Land had been mined for coal, copper, iron, and oil. The money made in these enterprises was available for investment or real-estate speculation, new inventions, and the stock market.

The Big Issues

As the war ended and the soldiers began to return home, two major issues faced the federal government. One centered on who had the authority to design the plan for restoring the Union. Was it the executive branch (the President) or was it the legislative branch (Congress)?

The other major issue was whether to readmit the seceded states to the Union. Some Republicans believed that the southern states lost their rights when they seceded and should be treated as conquered territory. This same group, called the Radical Republicans, also believed that blacks should be given full civil rights, including the right to vote.

Some northerners, however, insisted that one of the reasons the war had been fought was to prove that secession was illegal. Therefore, those states that had "seceded" had really been part of the Union all along, and they still had the same rights and privileges as the northern states. This view was obviously held by the South as well.

For years, Grant had believed that a military man should not be involved in politics. But now events were forcing him to take sides. When a grand jury in Virginia tried to charge General Lee with treason, Lee appealed to Grant. Grant went to President Johnson and made it very clear that under the terms of the surrender agreement, Lee could never be charged with treason. Johnson and others backed down and the charge against Lee was dropped.

GRANT ENTERS POLITICS

By August of 1867, Edwin Stanton, the secretary of war, had become closely allied with the Radical Republicans. Annoyed beyond endurance by Stanton's lack of loyalty, Johnson asked Stanton to resign from the Cabinet. When he refused, Johnson suspended him and offered Grant the position.

This request put Grant in a terrible bind. If he refused, someone else might take the position and do such a good job that Grant would have to share some of the popularity he was enjoying.

To refuse the position and retire would also be taking a step backward—an act that Grant never liked to do. As a compromise, Johnson offered him the position on a "part-time" basis: Grant would remain a general but he would also serve as a Cabinet member. At last, Grant had made the big step—he had entered the world of politics.

Grant was to find politics much more difficult than warfare. As commander-in-chief of his armies, he could make decisions and carry them out with little interference from the public or Congress—as long as he was successful. But in politics, he was to learn that any decision he made would adversely affect some group of people or some cause.

Caught in the Middle

When Johnson asked Grant, as acting secretary of war, to remove General Philip Sheridan as a commander of one of the southern military districts, Grant at first refused because he knew Sheridan was a capable and fair administrator. However, Johnson chose to invoke the constitutional right of a President, as commander-in-chief of the army, and forced Grant to request Sheridan's resignation.

The newspapers immediately accused Grant of being used by Johnson to defy the will of the people. Grant was caught in the crossfire, and there was no safe middle ground to take. Congress wanted to wrest control of the South from the President's hands, yet Johnson was determined to keep it by appointing military commanders he favored to control the southern districts.

Grant's uncomfortable position as acting secretary of war was finally resolved by another event. Earlier, over Johnson's veto, the Senate had passed the Tenure of Office Act, making it illegal for the President to remove certain federal offiiceholders without the approval of the Senate. (The act was declared unconstitutional by the Supreme Court in 1926.) The

Senate then used the Tenure of Office Act to retaliate against President Johnson and ordered the reinstatement of Stanton as secretary of war. This gave Grant the "out" he desperately wanted. He personally returned the keys of office to Stanton— an act that infuriated Johnson.

JOHNSON IMPEACHED

A short time later, the House of Representatives took a step *never* taken before—to impeach the President, or accuse him of illegal actions. If the accusations could be proven, the President would be removed from office. In the trial before the Senate, Johnson was acquitted by a single vote and remained in office.

Grant stayed clear of the impeachment proceedings. From the time the war ended, it was obvious that he could win either the Democratic or the Republican nomination for President. But the events leading up to Johnson's impeachment put Grant into the Republican camp. It was also the party of the majority of the men who fought in the Union armies. They were determined to have Grant as President—and he knew it!

THE REPUBLICANS PICK GRANT

At the Republican Party convention in Chicago in the spring of 1868 to select a presidential candidate for the elections in November, every delegate voted for Grant on the first ballot. When the representatives of the Republican Party called on him to formally accept the nomination, his brief speech included the comment, "I shall have no policy of my own to interfere against the will of the people." And his written acceptance ended with the words, "Let us have peace."

Perhaps it was words like these that led the voters to hope

Before the advent of radio and television, most publicity for political candidates was done with campaign posters. This one advertises the Republican ticket of Grant and Colfax for the election of 1868. (Library of Congress.)

that Grant's presidency would end sectional strife and political disorder. It was unfortunate that Grant was not equal to the task.

Grant took no active part in the election campaign and returned to Galena to await the returns. In the popular vote, Grant won by 300,000. It was the black vote of 450,000 that gave him this majority.

In his inaugural address, Grant made two significant statements. He urged ratification of the 15th Amendment, which guaranteed blacks the right to vote. He also expressed a concern about the need for proper treatment of the Indians and a hope that they would eventually be granted citizenship. With the formal inauguration ceremony over, Julia and Ulysses Grant, with their family, proceeded to the White House.

PRESIDENT GRANT INHERITS A MESS

A new nation had emerged from the chaos of the Civil War, but it was not quite the nation that Lincoln had envisioned. The dream of a country where all men and women are treated equally and have the right to vote and participate in government would indeed be a long time in coming. Perhaps, had Johnson and Grant been men with deeper insights into the presidential role, the dream might have been realized sooner. It is hard to say because so many factors made the Reconstruction Era a time of great turmoil.

Various groups sought to gain power in order to promote their own interests. The Radical Republicans of the North were determined to continue as the party in power, and they sought new voter strength among the newly freed blacks. Southern planters and businessmen were trying to regain some of the wealth and power they had enjoyed before the war. In states where whites outnumbered blacks, the Democratic Party was trying to make a comeback.

There was one more ingredient in the mess Grant inherited. The disruption of the war and the rise of big business had enabled corrupt and incompetent men to gain positions of power at all levels of government—federal, state, and local.

GRANT'S LIMITATIONS

It was Ulysses Grant's misfortune to become President at such a difficult time. Basically, he was ill-prepared for the job. He lacked knowledge of the law and the Constitution; he had rarely voted in an election. His only experience in understanding the relationship between the presidency and Congress had been during the last two years of Johnson's administration. And he had little understanding of the new economic changes that were taking place in business and industry.

Both Ulysses and Julia regarded his election as a reward for service to his country during the war years. They also saw nothing wrong in accepting gifts of homes and furnishings from a grateful public. Had not countries like England showered rich awards on such military heroes as the Duke of Wellington? It did not dawn on Grant that those who contributed to these gifts might some day expect favors in return.

During the war years, Grant had displayed qualities of consistency, honesty, and decision. These had served him well when dealing with men who were expected to jump at his commands. As President, he failed to see that he not only had to lead, but to win the support of the people and Congress in order to achieve his goals.

As general of the Union armies, he seemed to be a fine judge of the men under his command. Yet, when it came to politics, his judgment proved faulty. Often, he stubbornly defended men who used and abused his friendship for their own political or financial gain.

GRANT PICKS A CABINET

Grant's selection of a Cabinet revealed just how naive and inexperienced he was. Two of his appointments went to his best friends. John Rawlins, who had served and advised him during and after the war, was made secretary of war. Elihu Washburne, the Illinois congressman who had been his mentor and pressed for Grant's military promotions, was made secretary of state. The latter, under an agreement with Grant, served for one week and was then appointed Minister to France. (The secretary of state position was simply to give Washburne added credentials when he went to France!) Hamilton Fish, a first-rate choice, then became secretary of state; he was the only Cabinet officer to serve Grant ably through his two terms in office.

Grant appointed several people whom he had not even bothered to ask and who had to be talked into taking the jobs after the announcements had been made. One man even proved ineligible for the position given him. Grant also failed to confer with or seek the advice of party members, and thus angered many of them. Moreover, he lost a golden opportunity to get started on the right foot with the members of Congress.

But Grant was a folk hero to the people. His personal popularity sustained him during his first months in office. Unfortunately, he did not use his power to provide forthright leadership during what is known as "the honeymoon period" (the first few months of a presidency).

GRANT'S PLANS FOR AMERICAN INDIANS

One of Grant's first acts as President was to make good on his inaugural promise to help the Indians. He named as Commissioner of Indian Affairs, General Ely S. Parker, the full-blooded Seneca Indian who had served as an aide to Grant through much of the war. A program called "Grant's Peace Policy" was intended to educate Indians and to treat them as individuals rather than merely as tribesmen. Grant had seen how successfully Parker had found a place for himself in American society. It was Grant's hope that other Indians would do as well.

SETBACK FOR BLACK CIVIL RIGHTS

For another group, the blacks, Grant's presidency was to be a downhill slide. By the time Grant entered the White House, all but three southern states had been readmitted into the Union. Despite the fact that military commands still held sway in the South, individual state legislatures were able to enact laws. The 15th Amendment, which gave blacks the right to vote, was ratified in March 1870. But it did not take long for southern legislators to pass laws limiting the freedom of the former slaves.

Terrorism was also used against blacks. One organization, called the Ku Klux Klan, wore white sheets and hoods to conceal the identity of white men who rode through the countryside burning homes, threatening lives, and often murdering and torturing blacks as well as some poor whites who dared to vote or talk about voting. Bloody race riots broke out in Louisiana and Mississippi. Before long, blacks, who had been voting and even serving in such high government positions as lieutenant governor, began to desert the polling booths.

The Ku Klux Klan Act of 1871 gave Grant the authority to investigate and prosecute cases. Over 1,000 men were convicted of terrorist crimes. Nor did Grant hesitate to use military force when needed.

Northerners were getting tired of paying the cost of both military intervention and solutions to the "southern question." So they were once again willing to let the South set up its own state governments. The Radical Republican influence died out as the blacks lost the right to vote. The Democratic Party took over and became so strong that it consistently delivered at election times a voting bloc that came to be known as "the solid South."

For the blacks, the door had been opened momentarily. They had glimpsed freedom and tasted the fruits of democracy. Education, poor though it might be, would henceforth be available to them. But it would take more than a century before they again achieved the dream that was snatched away from them during the Reconstruction Era.

Chapter 7
Life at the White House

Life for Ulysses was a series of peaks and valleys—or perhaps more like a roller coaster ride. Who could have foreseen when he left the leather shop and the little house in Galena in 1861 that eight years later the Grant family would be living in the White House! For Ulysses, it was the apex of his career. For Julia, it was the fulfillment of her social ambitions.

Though Julia was "new at the game," she learned quickly. The temperament of Mrs. Lincoln and the chronic illness of Mrs. Johnson had put a damper on White House hospitality for many years. But with the Grant family in residence, the White House became the center of Washington social life. Julia encouraged the friendship of Mrs. Hamilton Fish, a socialite with impeccable taste, and listened to her suggestions and advice. Mrs. Fish often served with Julia in the receiving line at White House functions.

Julia loved the public dinners and the state occasions. She often appeared at such functions dressed in long, black velvet gowns that she believed showed her shoulders and arms to advantage. Such affairs were quite another matter for Ulysses. He would stand for a time and greet his guests. But on his face he wore a grim expression that seemed to say, "I'll fight this to the end."

Julia Dent Grant posed for this photograph by Matthew Brady while she lived in the White House as the First Lady. (Library of Congress.)

THE GRANT CHILDREN

It had been years since the White House had rung out with as much noise and frivolity. Ten-year-old Jesse, the family clown, managed to charm and get everyone to do his bidding, from his parents to cabinet members. One time, when special stamps he had ordered from a stamp dealer had not arrived, young Jesse sought the advice of the Cabinet. After much debate, the group decided that Jesse should ask the White House policeman to write a letter to the delinquent dealer.

When Julia decided that Jesse needed the company of children his own age, she gathered six boys in the gardener's tool shed. The group formed their own secret club and provided companionship for Jesse. Scampering through the corridors of the White House, they also added to the noise level.

Ulysses S. Grant, Jr., their second son, was affectionately known as "Buck" because he had been born in Ohio, the Buckeye State. Buck entered Harvard just as the family began life in the White House. He spent several years at Harvard and then began a career in banking. Any success he had was due to knowing "the right people," though Julia and Ulysses thought he was a financial genius. Nor would later events change their minds about him.

Fred, the oldest son, was appointed by President Johnson to the military academy at West Point. Hardly a credit to the family name, he ranked last in discipline out of a class of 41 and did equally as bad in his academic subjects. No wonder that Democrats accused Grant of favoritism when, shortly after graduation, Fred accompanied his father's old friend, General of the Army William Sherman, on a tour of duty in Europe.

During the period when Julia and Ulysses were raising their children, Americans believed that children should be treated according to two rules: "Spare the rod and spoil the child," and "Children should be seen but not heard." By such standards, Julia and Ulysses were probably viewed as very indulgent parents. Ulysses never scolded or whipped his children, and they were always surrounded by great affection— quite a contrast with Grant's own upbringing! Even family dinners at the White House were relaxed affairs. The table conversation was always peppered with children's questions and Grant's patient responses.

The relationship between husband and wife was also an extremely affectionate one. On more than one occasion during the war, Julia had risked her life to be with her husband. His spirits and his energy always seemed to revive upon her arrival. Even at the White House, they could be seen holding hands, much like young lovers.

Among the children, Nellie was probably Grant's favorite. She entered the White House as a typical 13-year-old teenager and quickly blossomed into the White House princess. For more than 25 years, there had not been a young girl at the executive mansion, so a sentimental America gobbled up news of everything she said and did. When she was 15 years old, Nellie stayed very late at a cotillion, or ball, and some newspapers clucked disapprovingly. Julia, though disturbed by the criticism, was nevertheless pleased by all the attention her daughter was receiving.

THE DENTS AND THE GRANTS

The White House was also home for the widowed Grandpa Dent, the old colonel of White Haven. Still the strong supporter of the South, he stalked the halls insulting Yankees and berating the acts of the Radical Republicans.

Grandfather Jesse Grant was almost a permanent guest. He had been appointed postmaster of Covington, Kentucky, his hometown, but he spent most of his time trying to bolster his own importance by explaining to visitors how much influence he had with the President.

Other Dents and Grants flowed in and out of the executive mansion. For some unknown reason, the only member of the family who did not attend the inauguration or ever visit the White House was Hannah Grant, the President's mother.

The postwar years were a time when people seemed more interested in making money than encouraging the arts and culture. Certainly Grant had little interest in either. The President had no eye for art and no ear for music, though he was reputed to appreciate the beauty of flowers. Even his appreciation of gourmet food was limited. The only meat he would eat was beef, and the longer it was cooked, the better he liked it. He disliked fowl of any kind and boasted that he would not eat "anything that went on two legs."

A WHITE HOUSE WEDDING

By the spring of 1872, Julia decided that perhaps Nellie was getting a bit too sophisticated. Millionaire friends of the Grants, the Bories, were planning a trip abroad and invited Nellie to join them. (Borie had served as Grant's first secretary of the navy.) Both mother and daughter took them up on the suggestion.

In England, Nellie was treated as royalty. She was presented to Queen Victoria and enjoyed the experience immensely. She was entertained at garden parties and met much of British society. To make the fairy tale complete, Nellie, on the boat returning from England, fell in love with a young Englishman, Algernon Sartoris, son of minor gentry. By the time the boat landed, young Algernon had proposed.

At age 18, Nellie was married in the East Room of the White House in what the newspapers described as "a quiet wedding." Forty members of the Marine band played softly for the 200 guests. During the ceremony, the normally impassive President "looked steadfastly at the floor and wept."

GRANT'S CODE OF FRIENDSHIP

After 40 years as a "loner," Grant now found himself surrounded by friends. One of the cardinal rules of his life was a binding loyalty and devotion to his friends. Because he continued to give appointments to his friends and relatives, he was often accused of "nepotism," of "taking care of his own," rather than appointing the best person for the job.

Stories about his loyalty to old friends delighted the American public. But when the public found Grant's loyalties were misplaced, people were quick to condemn his poor judgment.

Chapter 8

The Bubble Bursts

During his presidency, rarely did Grant take the initiative and show political leadership. One of the few times he did so was over the issue of annexation of the Dominican Republic (formerly Santo Domingo). Annexation had originally been the idea of William Seward, who had served as secretary of state under Johnson. Seward, like many others, believed that it was the destiny of the United States to expand beyond its present borders. He had arranged the purchase of Alaska from Russia, annexed the Midway Islands, west of Hawaii, and was looking at ways the United States could expand into the Caribbean when Grant was inaugurated.

The Dominican Republic occupies two-thirds of Hispaniola, an island in the Caribbean. Haiti, a former French colony, occupies the other third of the island. For many years, the Dominican Republic had endured internal strife and corruption. Two American adventurers living there encouraged the Dominican President, Bonaventure Baez, to send an emissary to Washington to discuss the possibility of annexation by the United States. An interview with Grant was arranged.

By the time the emissary left Washington, Grant was convinced that annexation was an excellent idea. The Dominican Republic would be an excellent place for settlement of newly freed blacks! The land was rich and had ex-

A full-length photograph of Grant that was taken during his presidency. He was no longer the slim military man that he used to be while in the army. (Library of Congress.)

cellent mineral resources. Three or four black states could be carved out of the island — states that would become part of the Union.

PLAYING THE POLITICIAN

The task of negotiating agreements between the United States and other countries is customarily left to the secretary of state. But Grant bypassed Secretary Hamilton Fish and sent instead his personal secretary, Orville Babcock, to the island to meet with President Baez and draw up a treaty of annexation. However, when the document was delivered to the members of Grant's Cabinet, they were given little opportunity to discuss its merits.

Grant decided to play politician and marshall his own support for the Dominican Republic project. On the first Sunday in January of 1870, he went to the home of Senator Charles Sumner, who, though dining with two newspapermen, graciously invited the President in. Quietly Grant explained the nature of his visit. The three men were shocked. No President had ever come, hat in hand, to ask a powerful senator for his support of a project! When Grant left that evening, he was fairly certain that he had Sumner's support.

During the months that followed, Grant was to learn otherwise. The newspapers began to leak stories about the unscrupulous speculators who had instigated the project. Reports were published by Baez's enemies describing his ruthless violations of the little country's Constitution.

Grant worked hard to muster allies for his cause. He made it his business to meet with the most prominent senators. Even young Jesse remembered how troubled his father had been during those "strangely tense days" when the Senate debate was in progress.

On a steamy day in June, with senators anxious to leave

the stifling capital, the treaty was brought to a vote—and voted down. Grant's vision of himself as a strong President, leading the country as he had led his armies, suffered a severe blow.

CIVIL SERVICE REFORM

"To the victor belongs the spoils!" Those words, first spoken by President Andrew Jackson, frankly described the way people were appointed to positions in the U.S. government. From the lowliest clerk to the heads of departments, men and women were routinely hired and fired on the basis of party loyalty, and little thought was paid to the talents or the ethical conduct of the appointees. When Democrats came into power, Republican civil servants were dismissed and replaced by Democrats. This procedure was reversed when Republicans came into power.

During his first term of office, Grant had witnessed bribery and corruption on the part of wealthy businessmen and respected members of Congress. If these men could be "bought," it was even easier for those in customs offices, tax bureaus, and land offices to be bribed. Moreover, people who worked hard and had talent were not rewarded. Even worse, if a new administration came into power, they were in danger of losing their jobs.

A civil service based on merit was not Grant's idea but that of Senator Charles Sumner, who had introduced a bill in 1864 to establish such a system. His fellow legislators had regarded it as just another of Sumner's moral but impractical ideas. Grant, however, sensed a strong demand for government reform. In his second inaugural message, he denounced the spoils system. He urged the passage of a law that would make a person's ability and conduct the test for getting and keeping a government job. Congress appointed a commission, headed by George William Curtis, to look into the matter.

The commission recommended that all jobs be classified. Positions were to be filled from a list of applicants who had passed examinations. Promotions, too, were to be based on tests. The President asked Congress to pass legislation and appropriate funds for the program.

While waiting for Congress to act, Grant fired 192 officials who had been found guilty of corruption or inefficiency. But Grant's efforts in this area were to come to nothing. Congress refused to appropriate the necessary funds, and the recommendations of the commission were ignored. In 1875, Curtis resigned, weary of fighting those who persisted in appointing public servants according to party affiliation. It was not until 1883 that a merit system of civil service was finally voted into law.

GREELEY VERSUS GRANT

In 1872, a coalition of Democrats and Republican liberals nominated Horace Greeley, a liberal editor of the *New York Tribune,* as their candidate for President. While Greeley toured the country, an unusual procedure for a presidential candidate at that time, Grant spent the summer at the family home in Long Branch, New Jersey. He told a friend, "Two presidential candidates were public speakers and both were beaten. I am no speaker and I don't want to be beaten." He was not!

In the North, the slogan "Vote as you fought" appealed to Union veterans. And with Radical Republicans enforcing control of the Ku Klux Klan, blacks in the South came to the polls in sufficient numbers to carry all the reconstructed states for Grant except Georgia and Texas.

But as Grant embarked on his second term of office, he was a bit more humble about the job. The *New York Tribune* described his second inaugural address as "the utterances of

Whoever designed this Republican poster for the 1872 election campaign played up Grant and Wilson's roles as men who worked with their hands. The poster is not quite accurate. Although Grant worked for his father's tannery business, he refused to do the work of a tanner. (Library of Congress.)

a man of the best intentions profoundly desirous to govern wisely and justly and profoundly ignorant of the means of which good government is secured."

History was to bear out the truth of that statement.

THE PANIC OF 1873

Julia and Ulysses had barely settled into their second term in the White House when the country faced one of the greatest financial crises of all time. The huge sums of money made by many businessman and speculators in the postwar years had led everyone to believe that the "boom" would continue. But money had shifted from the production of goods to speculation in railroads, oil fields, and gold and silver mines. For years, there had been an unfavorable balance of trade with foreign countries. More goods were being imported than exported. Europe was already in the midst of a depression, and European investors were getting rid of American stocks to pay their own debts. As a result, American stock prices were falling.

In the United States there had been so much agricultural expansion in the West that there was a surplus of crops. Farm prices were falling.

On September 17, Grant was dining with his good friend, Jay Cooke, at Cooke's country home in Pennsylvania. During the evening, the white-bearded banker received a series of urgent messages but never interrupted the elegant dinner and the pleasantries to tell the President what those messages were about. Not until the next day, when Grant returned to Washington, did he discover that the banking house of Jay Cooke and Company had closed its doors.

Following the collapse of Cooke's banking company, which had financed both the war and the building of the Northern Pacific Railroad, the Panic of 1873 began. Within two days, stocks had fallen so dramatically that the Stock Market Exchange also closed. People rushed to withdraw their money from banks. Factory after factory was forced to shut down. Many people lost their jobs, and long bread lines began to appear in cities.

Bankers, brokers, railroad men, and merchants besieged Grant and his new secretary of the treasury, William A. Richardson, with advice, requests, and suggestions. Speculators wanted to get business moving again. They urged the printing of more currency in order to get more money into circulation. Conservatives were afraid that such actions would lead to inflation and higher prices. In January 1874, however, Congress voted 125–98 to support the inflationary measure.

Senator George F. Hoar urged the President to veto the money bill that Congress was preparing. "Well," replied Grant, "if you send it to me, make it just as bad as you can." Congress was shocked when Grant courageously vetoed the bill.

Grant had sensed correctly that conservative bankers and farmers would be up in arms if the measure passed. Even the *New York Tribune* called Grant's veto "a wise, courageous executive act." The popularity of Grant's veto forced Congress to work to create a more conservative measure that the President signed. But there was no "quick-fix" for the economic problems that plagued the nation. The depression that followed the Panic of 1873 lasted beyond Grant's years in the White House.

The Final Blows

The blows that did the most damage to Grant's reputation were dealt by those he trusted the most. The postwar problems of Reconstruction and the economy would have existed no matter who headed the government. But the corruption that persisted during his administration might not have been so flagrant had Grant been a less trusting and naive man.

During Grant's first term in office, his secretary of the navy accumulated a fortune by selling business contracts. The U.S. Minister to Brazil defrauded the government of $50,000 and fled to Europe. In Washington, D.C., the head of the Board of Public Works, through graft, ran up a debt of 17 million dollars. To the horror of taxpayers, Grant appointed the man governor of the District.

All of this was bad enough, but worse was still to come. For years, there had been rumors of a "Whisky Ring" composed of distillers (producers of whisky) and officials in the Treasury Department's Bureau of Internal Revenue. The members of the Whisky Ring conspired to defraud the government of part of its taxes on liquor. No attempts were made to expose those involved in the conspiracy until a new and energetic secretary of the treasury, Benjamin Bristow, was appointed to the Cabinet. When Grant learned of Bristow's investigation, he said, "Let no guilty man escape."

But most of them did escape—one, General Orville Babcock, with Grant's help. Babcock had been Grant's private secretary and trusted friend during Civil War days. In his position in the White House, Babcock was able to alert the "ring" of impending investigations. When the evidence against Babcock was brought to the President's attention, Babcock admitted nothing. Instead, he convinced Grant that Secretary Bristow was using the investigations to discredit Grant and gain the presidency for himself.

Grant gave a statement supporting Babcock and proclaimed him innocent. The statement was read into Babcock's trial, and Babcock was acquitted. Bristow, in disgust, resigned a few months later.

Julia wished to have her sons, Fred and Buck, close by during the remaining months of their White House stay. At her request, Ulysses appointed his sons as personal secretaries and thereby incurred further charges of nepotism.

Chapter 9

From the White House to Windsor Castle

Julia first read it in the newspapers. She could not quite believe that Ulysses had made the decision without first telling her. No third term! No more years in her lovely White House! "I'm sorry," Ulysses commented wryly. "You'll just have to settle for being an ex-first lady."

There was little doubt that Grant had been seriously contemplating a third term because he had no military pension and no job or business to which he could return. Whether it was the eruption of the Whisky Ring scandal three weeks earlier or the Republican defeats in the spring elections in Connecticut, on the eve of a convention of Pennsylvania Republicans, he decided not to run again.

"I do not want it anymore than I did the first . . . I would not accept a nomination even if it were tendered unless it should come under such circumstances as to make it an imperative duty." It is interesting to note that the last few words left the door open for a future demand for his services.

In December 1876, the hundredth anniversary of the

Declaration of Independence, Grant delivered his final State of the Union message to Congress. He began with an apology: "It was my fortune, or misfortune, to be called to the office of Chief Executive without any previous political training. Under such circumstances, it is but reasonable to suppose that errors of judgment must have occurred." He then went on to review the eight years of his administration.

The newspapers had little to say about the President's last annual message. The *New York Tribune* did comment, "The message is that of a man who is weary of public life and tired of political strife." And Grant probably was.

GRANT'S ACHIEVEMENTS AS PRESIDENT

Yet, looking back, Grant could have taken pride in his political accomplishments. He had helped the nation survive the Reconstruction Era, one of the most difficult periods with which a U.S. President has had to deal. He was the first President to seek a humane policy for the American Indian and the first to use the principle of arbitration to solve international conflicts. He heartily endorsed passage of the 15th Amendment and badgered Congress to pass the Ku Klux Klan Act, which was designed to protect the rights of blacks.

Grant's own attitude towards his efforts as President were summed up in his last message: "I have acted in every instance from a conscientious desire to do what was right, constitutional, within the law, and for the very best interests of the whole people. Failures have been errors of judgment, not of intent." As always with Grant, his heart was in the right place.

Julia Grant was not about to let her last days in the White House fade into oblivion. She was determined that her husband's administration would end on a grand scale. On New

Year's Day, 1877, a heavy snowfall could not deter throngs of well-wishers from calling at the White House. There, Julia proudly presented her youngest guest, Miss Julia Grant. The little daughter of son Fred had been born at the executive mansion six months earlier. Many years later, granddaughter Julia was to become the Princess Cantacuzene and be invited as a guest to the White House.

A SECRET INAUGURATION

Julia may have been concerned about making a final social splash, but Ulysses was more concerned that there be no slip in inaugurating the new President, Rutherford B. Hayes. Julia had planned a sumptuous dinner for Saturday evening, March 3rd, to which the newly elected Hayes had been invited. Grant's term of office ended officially on March 4th and the official inauguration was set for Monday, March 5th. But because the election results had been so close and so disputed, Grant feared that even a Sunday without a President might have disastrous consequences.

That evening, Grant sent his son Buck to find a Bible. He then asked President-elect Hayes and Morrison Waite, Chief Justice of the Supreme Court, to join him in the Red Room of the White House. There, in secret, Hayes took the oath of office as 19th President of the United States. Grant's presidency was over!

Shortly after the inauguration, the Grants left Washington. As the train pulled out of the station, they waved to their friends on the platform. Then Julia hurried to their compartment, where Ulysses found her crying.

"I feel like such a waif," she sobbed.

"Is that all?" he replied. "I thought something had happened. You must not forget that I am a waif, too."

WANDERLUST AND WORLD ACCLAIM

"I've always wanted to roam the world! What better time than now!" Ulysses' eyes sparkled as he spoke. It had been a long time since Julia and young Jesse had seen Ulysses so excited.

"There is nothing to hold us here," he went on. Turning to Jesse, Grant added, "And you're welcome to join us, if you would like." This exchange had taken place during their last Christmas at the White House. With Jesse home from college, the President had seized the opportunity to share an idea that had been percolating in his mind for some time.

Though Ulysses had indeed travelled far since his boyhood expeditions in Ohio and Kentucky, his wanderlust still was not satisfied. There was so much of the world that he and Julia had not seen. Now there was no war, no profession, no political appointment to hold them in the country. And there were savings and investments that would enable them to travel for two years. Buck was in charge of his father's investments and there seemed to be sufficient income to allow them to travel as they pleased. Grant thought $25,000 would be sufficient for the journey . . . a gross underestimate.

In May 1877, the steamship *Indiana* sailed from the harbor at Philadelphia with private citizens Ulysses, Julia, and Jesse Grant aboard. But it was not as private citizens that they were received all over the world. Nor was it ex-President Grant whom the public came to see. It was General Grant, the greatest soldier of his day.

There could not have been a grander send-off than the Grants had. Friends from their army and White House days gave them a bon voyage luncheon. Small boats, decorated with brilliantly colored pennants, lined the river. The sounds of cheers rose from the escort boats. Ship whistles and horns played across the water. The Grants were on their way!

On board with them was a reporter from the *New York Herald,* John Russell Young. The newspaper scented news in the travels of the Grants and Young's reports were to keep Grant's name alive with the American public for the next two years.

During the trans-Atlantic journey, Ulysses smoked cigars constantly and sometimes ate two lunches a day. He "never felt better." It was Julia who got seasick.

England Throws a Party

Their journey abroad began with tumultuous welcomes by the people of Liverpool, Manchester, and Newcastle, England. Thousands of cheering workers poured into the streets. Church bells rang out. Banners declared, "Let Us Have Peace." The people remembered the words of Grant's acceptance speech when he was first nominated for the presidency.

Grant responded simply, "I am a man of peace. I have always advocated peace. I never willingly, though I have gone through two wars, advocated war."

There is no doubt that he meant those words, for during his trip, he refused to review troops or a military parade.

Why did the working people of England come out by the thousands to welcome Grant? To them, Grant was the general who had led the war to free the slaves. They saw the war as a parallel to their own struggle against the wealthy mill owners and English high society. They saw in Grant the tanner's son who had achieved the highest office in the "land of opportunity." They saw in him their own strivings and hopes, and they loved and appreciated him for his successes and his failures.

However, not all of England was as taken by the Grant family. Their visit to Windsor Castle left Queen Victoria with some strong feelings about the manners of Americans, who knew little and cared less about English royal customs.

The Queen had issued to Julia and Ulysses an invitation to supper in her private dining room, a far greater compliment than a formal state dinner. Like any good American family, the Grants brought along their son, or as Julia described Jesse to the Queen, "our pet." But neither 20-year-old Jesse, nor Grant's friend, the American Consul General, Adam Badeau, had been invited.

When the Grant family retired to their rooms at the palace to dress for dinner, they learned that Jesse and Badeau would be dining with the "Household." Though it was carefully explained that the "Household" was not servants, Jesse, with Badeau egging him on, began to act like a 10-year-old. He raised such a fuss that two lords and two ladies were dispatched to the Queen to negotiate a peace. Sadly, Grant sympathized with his son's demands. The Queen, ever the lady, asked Jesse to dine "with the family."

The meal was coldly formal. Afterwards, the Queen spoke graciously to all her guests, even Jesse, whom she later described as "a very ill-mannered young Yankee." The Queen retired at 10 o'clock, and the Grants left the next morning without seeing her again.

In Scotland, Ulysses was greeted as a distinguished son by the clan of Grant. In Rome, he was received by the Pope. On the way to the reception, he passed through the galleries of great Vatican art, without stopping to admire any of the works. They visited the ruins of ancient Pompeii. Upon seeing the canals and waterways of Venice, he commented, "This would be a pretty city if they would only drain it!"

They criss-crossed the European continent without any set plans. When they wearied of castles and cathedrals, the Grants moved on.

Grant may not have appreciated the art and history of Europe, but he gained an appreciation of Europe's technical progress. He delighted in the bathrooms and fixtures of modern hotels and steamships. He was intrigued by bridges, railroads, and sewers. He represented the American interest in "what makes business work."

Grant was also a people-watcher. He loved to walk the streets of the cities by himself, observing the men and women as they went about their daily lives. Yet for all the accolades given him by the common people in England and throughout Europe, Ulysses did not really understand their plight. Nor did they know that he had, during his presidency, allied himself with the wealthy industrialists. He had very little understanding of the business world. He failed to see that the wealth of his friends was built upon the miserably low wages and oppressive working conditions of the men and women who toiled in the factories, railroads, and mines.

In 1877, at the very time that Grant was accepting the cheers of the English working class, a massive railroad strike was spreading in the United States. Workers were striking against the cut in wages imposed by the Hayes Administration. Grant's reaction to news of the strike was, "The strike should have been put down with a strong hand so it will not occur for another generation." It was.

In January 1878, the family arrived in Cairo and travelled up the Nile. Pictures show Julia garbed in the heavy clothes of the day, with her head swathed in veils to protect her as she ventured into the desert. She rode sidesaddle on a donkey past ancient villages, with parched, brown fields, brought on by a drought. They journeyed to the Holy Land and Constantinople, then back to Europe and a visit with Prince Otto von Bismarck.

The Meeting with Bismarck

Ulysses deemed his meeting with Bismarck as one of the greatest moments of their world tour. Yet when Ulysses called on the most powerful man in Europe, he displayed an American disdain for European formality. Situated in a nearby hotel, Ulysses decided to walk the short distance. He casually sauntered into the courtyard of Radziwell Palace. When the surprised guards on duty saw Grant, they snapped to attention and saluted. He tossed away his half-smoked cigar and briskly returned the salute. If Jefferson could walk to his inauguration, Grant could walk to Bismarck's palace!

Reporter Young's notes of the meeting attest that the two men discussed the Civil War, an assassination attempt on the life of Emperor Wilhelm, and the success of the Prussian Army in the Franco-Prussian War. For Bismarck, Grant broke his pledge not to review troops.

This meeting was followed a few days later by a dinner invitation to the palace. Julia, in her *Memoirs,* described how Prince Bismarck bent low over her hand and kissed it. She wrote, "I was, of course, enchanted with Prince Bismarck." Julia's fondest dreams were being realized.

THE GRANTS TOUR THE ORIENT

Their travels continued—to India, Burma, Siam, and Indo-China. In Canton, China, they were transported on sedan chairs to the palace of the governor-general. In Tientsin, he met the "Bismarck of the East," General Li Hung Chang. Li was so impressed with Grant that he asked him to carry a message to Japan. That message was to lead eventually to the opening of negotiations between China and Japan.

The Grants were enchanted with Japan. They were taken into the Imperial Palace, a place forbidden to the outside world. There they met Emperor Mutsubito and Empress Haruko. The emperor was himself a military leader. His high esteem for Grant was shown by his relaxation of formal court procedure that evening. To have received Grant was in itself a revolution. Even more so was the emperor's greeting of

On his trip around the world in 1877, Grant visited the Viceroy of China, Li Hung Chang. (Library of Congress.)

Grant with a handshake. Such a thing had never happened before in the history of Japanese royalty.

The Grants were impressed by the cleanliness of the people and the beauty of the land. Ulysses noted how the people were beginning to copy material things from America. He began to toy with the idea of Japan as a new market for American investments.

The newspaper accounts of the Grants' journey provided more than just material for a book by John Russell Young. (The book, a lavender-bound volume, was entitled *Around the World with General Grant*.) The newspaper coverage kept Grant's name on the lips of his countrymen—his hobnobbing with kings, queens, emperors, and maharajahs tickled the American public and enhanced his reputation.

All through his travels, Grant received news from home. The longer he stayed away, the more he heard about the failings of the Hayes Administration. The old Grant days glowed brighter by comparison. His friends begged him to put off his return until closer to election time. Perhaps if he did . . .

HOME AGAIN

But Julia was homesick and anxious to be reunited with the family. In September 1879, they arrived in San Francisco. Looking back, historians have noted that had Grant delayed his return for six more months, he might have captured the Republican nomination in 1880.

From September to January, the Grants moved slowly eastward, attending banquets and parades everywhere they went. The honors and attention he had received abroad gave Ulysses new esteem in the eyes of his countrymen and, in some respects, in his own eyes as well. He had responded to so many speeches and banquet toasts that he felt more comfortable with public speaking. His experiences with other countries and cultures gave him a worldly perspective. It may have been a limited perspective, but it was more than any other President had up to that time.

At each stop, Grant was invariably asked about his future plans. He refused to say anything on the subject. Once more, he was reluctant to risk seeking a position which he might fail to get. Yet he knew he needed employment. They could afford to live in Galena on the money they had, but they could not afford to live in a big city, such as New York or Philadelphia, in the style to which Julia had become accustomed.

The wave of enthusiasm for Grant as President crested too soon. By the time of the convention, the opposition had time to marshall their forces. Newspapers had begun to criticize Grant's appearance at every reception and parade. People were tiring of attending functions in his honor.

Grant was nominated, and on the first ballot he had the highest number of votes but not enough to win. All day Monday and through Tuesday morning the balloting went on— 26, 30, 36. In the end, however, Grant lost. The nomination went to James Garfield.

Deeply hurt, Grant was reluctant to campaign on Garfield's behalf. But when Garfield sent him a letter requesting his help, Grant did not refuse. His new skills as a speaker gave him confidence in discussing the issues that he felt were important. Grant's efforts undoubtedly played a part in Garfield's successful run for the presidency. But Grant's days as a politician were over.

Chapter 10
The Measure of a Man

It would have been a perfect day for a leisurely stroll. New York shows off its best weather in May. But this Sunday afternoon, the bearded, top-hatted gentleman had rushed the short distance by carriage. Favoring a lame foot, Grant stepped from the carriage and struggled up the steps of the Vanderbilt mansion.

The mission was one of the saddest and most difficult Grant ever had to perform. How did one ask a friend for $150,000?

FINANCIAL DISASTER

The years between Garfield's election and this day in 1884 had been a period of relative calm. Ulysses and Julia had settled into a fine home off Fifth Avenue in New York City, a home given to him by a group of wealthy friends. He had an office on Wall Street. Yet none of Grant's financial adventures, particularly in railroads, had paid off. By 1883, he was at loose ends and still not financially secure.

Two years earlier, Grant's son Buck had entered into a partnership with Ferdinand Ward, a rising star on Wall Street. The company books showed that Buck was now well on his way to becoming a millionaire. Buck suggested that Ulysses invest $100,000 in Grant and Ward. Not only did Grant invest, but so did other family members and friends.

The venture had seemed so profitable, so sound. For the first time in his life, Ulysses was able to give Julia $1,000 a month, with no questions asked. He was able to write a check without worrying about being overdrawn. It was a fool's paradise.

The brokerage house of Grant and Ward was using their clients' securities, such as stocks and bonds, to borrow money from banks. But the company was pledging the same securities to support more than one bank loan. In May 1884, the company was asked to pay off some of its loans. The game was up! Ward begged Ulysses to borrow the money to cover the debt.

William Henry Vanderbilt, the railroad tycoon who had built the New York Central, gave Ulysses the loan. "To tell the truth," he said, "I care very little about Grant and Ward. But to accommodate you personally, I will draw my check for the amount you ask. I consider it a personal loan to you and not to any other party." Vanderbilt was one of the most admiring of the millionaires who were friends of Grant.

But it was not enough. In a few days, all of Wall Street learned that Ward had disappeared and that the Grant and Ward securities were worthless. Worst of all, the Grant name was now associated with a Wall Street swindle. Grant had been "taken" before, but he had never been swindled of his reputation.

That night, he and Julia sat and glumly reviewed their assets. Ulysses had $81 in his wallet. Between her purse and the cookie jar, Julia had $130. Once more, the Grants would have to start all over again.

Julia proceeded to sell two small houses they had in Washington. Ulysses sold off his horses and carriages. To pay off his debt, Grant deeded his New York home to Vanderbilt, as well as his wartime trophies and many presents that he had received. Among these treasures were a gold medal from Congress; campaign swords that had been presented by grateful soldiers and citizens; jade, porcelain, and a teak cabinet, gifts from Li Hung Chang, the Chinese statesman; and elephant tusks from the King of Siam. Vanderbilt later presented these gifts to the United States government. Several friends also left checks on the hall table after visiting the Grants. All were paid back as soon as Grant began to earn money.

Years earlier, Grant's father had complained, "West Point spoiled my son for business." Ulysses' latest financial ventures seemed to prove Jesse right once more. Again, his life had taken a turn for the worse. The family was living on borrowed money in their summer home at Long Branch, New Jersey. Once more, Julia managed the house and did the cooking. Except for the gleeful sounds of their grandchildren, the house seemed sad, depressed. But at age 62, Grant discovered a hidden talent and a new profession.

GRANT FIGHTS BACK

In January of 1884, Grant had been approached by *Century Magazine,* the leading magazine of its day, to write some articles describing his battles in the Civil War. General Sherman and others had written such articles, but Grant had never felt the need to do so. Besides, Grant had been riding high. He had a good income from his investments; his future seemed secure. Moreover, he had this strange compulsion that he must never retrace his steps. Reliving his war experiences would be retracing his steps.

Now there was no way out. Grant had to earn money. He had come back from his failures before and he could do it again. He had to regain financial security for his family. For this would be his last chance.

One day that summer, Grant topped off his lunch with

his favorite dessert, a juicy peach. As he tried to swallow the first bite, he gasped and clutched his throat. The pain was excruciating. Grant assumed it was a sore throat. What Grant was experiencing was an early symptom of what doctors would diagnose as cancer later that year.

Now it was imperative for Grant to find work, and the offer from *Century* was gratefully accepted. The success of his articles on Shiloh and Vicksburg encouraged him. Quietly, and without telling Julia, an idea was forming in his mind. He would write a book. Though he did not yet have a publisher, he began writing. His son, Fred, and his family were living with Julia and Ulysses. Fred had already written a book. It seemed only natural for him to assist with some of the research and details of his father's book.

Enter Mark Twain

Learning of the project, the publisher of Century Corporation made what seemed like a fair offer to Grant. But Lady Luck had not yet abandoned him. On November 18, 1884, a famous writer finished a lecture tour with a reading at Chickering Hall in New York City. It was a rainy evening. As he and his wife started walking through the mist, they heard, "Did you know General Grant has actually determined to write his memoirs and publish them?"

The author was Mark Twain. For years, he had been an admirer of Grant despite the fact that Twain had served for a short time as an "irregular Confederate." (He later confessed, "I could have become a soldier myself if I waited. I had got part of it learned. I knew more about retreating than the man who invented retreating.")

Grant, in turn, was an admirer of the author of *Huckleberry Finn* and *Tom Sawyer*. On his world tour, Grant had chuckled over Twain's *Innocents Abroad*. The two men had become close friends after they met at a banquet honoring

Grant in 1879. Twain had been the last speaker. He took the opportunity to make several hilarious comments about Grant that had an amazing effect on the man who had sat, straight-faced, through one speaker after another. As Twain described it, "I broke him up utterly! He laughed until his bones ached."

Now Twain was determined to take advantage of their friendship, to offer Grant a contract for his memoirs. Twain's timing could not have been better. The morning after the lecture, Twain rushed to the Grant home. Ulysses was once more settled in New York for the winter. Twain found Grant in the library with his son Fred.

According to Twain's account, Grant was just about to put his pen to a contract with Century. Twain told Fred to stop Ulysses and to read the contract aloud. Twain pretended outrage at the terms of the agreement. Grant could do far better . . . and Twain was the man to offer him far better terms. He now had his own publishing house, Charles L. Webster and Company, and he assured Grant that a two-volume set of his memoirs would be an instant best-seller.

Wary of all business deals now, Grant had Fred and a lawyer check on Twain's contract and company, as well as offers from other companies. Grant had some misgivings about accepting Twain's offer, because it was Century that had first come to him. In fact, Grant did give Century an opportunity to meet Twain's offer. But word about Grant's illness had already leaked out. Century was unwilling to make such an extravagant offer to a man who might die before the work was completed. Grant signed on with Twain's company.

THE FINAL BATTLE

All during that winter, Ulysses toiled at his desk. His writing had always been terse and clear, but it lacked vivid descriptions. Bit by bit, his style improved. There were many skeptics who wrote in newspapers and magazines that Grant was not actually doing his own writing. Yet seven days a week, four hours a day, Grant kept to his schedule. It was *his* book and *he* had to finish it.

Grant would sit with a stack of notes in one corner of his desk. Next to it was a card table with his maps. In bold crayon were marked the positions of the Confederate and Union troops. He wore large eyeglasses with hard, rubber rims and used a pencil to write because he did not want to interrupt the flow of his thoughts to dip a pen into ink.

There were days when he could barely summon the strength to sit in his chair. On his doctor's orders, Grant had given up cigars. Swallowing became so difficult that even sipping water caused severe pain. He still tried to join the family at meal times, but he had to steel himself to sip milk or cold soups. Sometimes the pain forced him to leave the table. There were more and more periods when he could not talk and was forced to write notes to Julia, Fred, and the doctors. The family helped in every way. They would sit in the evening chatting or reading aloud to Ulysses.

Mark Twain visited and helped to read and correct the proofs from the printer. But he made no comments about Grant's writing style. The general began to feel uneasy. Was he right in believing that the book was well-written? Ulysses expressed his concern to Fred, who conveyed the message to Twain.

Twain was shocked that the famed general needed assurance or encouragement. "I was as much surprised," Twain wrote, "as Columbus' cook would have been to learn that Columbus wanted his opinion as to how well Columbus was doing his navigating." What Twain had not realized was that Grant still needed praise to confirm his feelings about himself. Twain took the time to assure Grant that his writing was excellent, furthering the relationship between the two men.

Help from Congress

Grant had lived with the hope that Congress would see fit to reinstate him in the army. If he were, he would receive a lieutenant-general's salary and, at his death, Julia would receive a pension of $5,000. Early in 1885, the Senate passed such a bill, but it failed to pass the House by 16 votes. This was not the first time that such a bill had come before Congress.

By now, everyone knew that Grant's illness was fatal. Congress would adjourn March 4, 1885, and chances seemed slim for passing a bill to help Grant. At 12 noon that day, the new President, Grover Cleveland, and the new Congress would take over. Other bills were being debated. The Grant bill seemed doomed.

Just before 11 o'clock in the morning, the House was to vote on a disputed election between two candidates in Iowa. One of the men, James Wilson, rose and offered to cede the election if the House would consider the Grant bill. Wild cheering greeted the offer. With a voice vote, the bill was passed and rushed to the Senate. Most of the senators were readying themselves for the inauguration, but they rushed to the Senate chamber to vote "Aye." The outgoing President, Chester Arthur, delayed the inauguration long enough to sign the bill as his last act in office.

The nation had not forgotten Grant after all! Though he showed little reaction to the news, it had to be a source of comfort to the victor of Vicksburg.

Several times during the spring of 1885, newspapers reported Grant's death as imminent. In one of his notes to his doctor, he joked, "The *World* has been killing me off for a year and a half. If it does not change, it will get it right in time."

The disease was marked by good and bad periods. But

after each bad period, Grant had less strength. He lost more than 50 pounds and began to make plans for his death. He went over his will. Daily, he tried to keep up with the requests that poured across his desk. One day, while autographing pictures requested by his medical team, his son Fred shoved one more paper before him for a signature. It read:

> To the President of the United States:
> May I ask you to favor the appointment of Ulysses
> S. Grant (the son of my son, Frederick Grant) as
> a cadet at West Point upon his application. In do-
> ing so, you will gratify the wishes of
> Ulysses S. Grant

(Ulysses S. Grant, III was then three years old. He would graduate from West Point in 1903.)

FINAL DAYS

The Grants sold their home in Long Branch, New Jersey, in April 1885. As the heat in New York City became more oppressive, the doctors suggested a cooler climate with clean mountain air. Joseph W. Drexel, a member of the well-known banking family, offered the Grants use of his summer "cottage" (with about 12 rooms!) at Mount McGregor in the foothills of the Adirondack Mountains. It was gratefully accepted, as was the offer of William Vanderbilt's private railroad car to take them there.

On June 16, the family departed from Grand Central Station in New York City. The general's coat hung loosely on him, several sizes too big. His hair and beard were now snow-white. The train travelled up the Hudson River, and for the last time, Grant saw West Point. He had first made that journey more than 40 years earlier. All along the way, people lined up at the stations to catch a glimpse of their great hero. At Saratoga Springs, to the cheers of the people standing by, Grant walked unaided to the railroad car taking them up the mountain.

Once more, he settled in and returned to his work. The first volume of his memoirs had already been rushed to press. Advance sales left no doubt of its success. Though Grant would not live to see it, in February 1886, Julia would receive the largest royalty check ever written — $200,000.

Mark Twain arrived on June 27, hopeful that he could wrest the second volume from Ulysses. But Grant insisted that there were a few more passages that needed reworking. Time was running out and Ulysses was determined to put all the details of his life in order. He wrote a note to Fred with plans for his burial. He requested that whatever and wherever the tomb was, there would be a place for Julia beside him. Reading the note, Julia finally faced the reality of Ulysses' death. From that day on, she never left the cottage, not even for a walk or to play with her grandchildren. When she and Ulysses sat on the porch, their wicker chairs side by side, she held his hand, as if afraid to let go.

When Ulysses could no longer work at a desk, he sat in a chair with a clipboard or scratch pad in his lap. Clutching his pencil with whatever strength he had, he continued to commit his memories to paper. The writing was now scrawled and shaky, but his mind remained clear.

The finished book deals with Grant's early life, goes through the Mexican-American War, and concludes with the end of the Civil War. Whether he would have written about his years in the White House if he had lived long enough is questionable. Perhaps, in his eyes, the years of his presidency did not represent his finest hours, as did the four years of the Civil War. The book was not only a best-seller at the time, it continues to be printed today. It is a primary source of information for authors, researchers, and anyone interested in

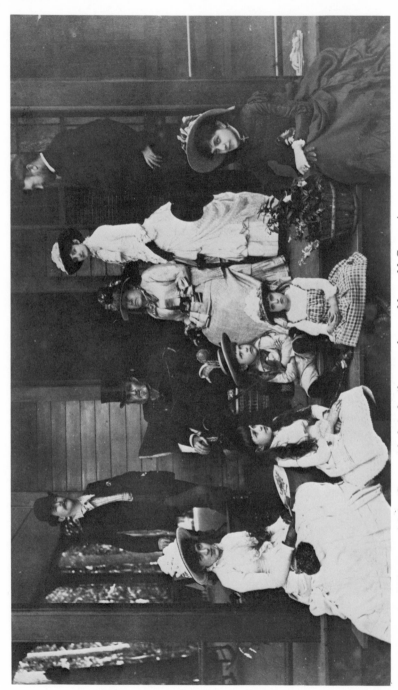

This photograph of Ulysses and Julia Grant with their family was taken at Mount McGregor in July 1885, the month that Ulysses died. (Library of Congress.)

the Civil War. Critics continue to praise Grant's writing for its simplicity and clarity.

The introduction to the book bears the date July 1, 1885, the day Ulysses completed the text. Working on the book had kept him alive, but now his work was done. Slowly, the last of his strength oozed away. All of his children were now at Mount McGregor—Nellie from England and the boys Fred, Buck, and Jesse—as were several of the grandchildren. And, of course, loving Julia, holding on desperately to their last few days together.

Ulysses died at 8:08 in the morning of July 23, 1885. His last wishes were met. He and Julia are buried in New York City, in a large tomb that overlooks the Hudson River. The words on the tomb are Grant's own: "Let us have peace."

EPILOGUE

The measure of a man is not how well he handles his success but how well he survives his failures. At age 39, Grant might well have been labeled a "loser." He had failed in the army, he had failed as a farmer, and he had failed as a businessman. In the following years, he would lose a nomination for the presidency, lose all his money, and be called a swindler.

But after each misfortune, Grant would pick himself up, dust himself off, and start all over again. In the end, he won the highest elected office in his country, world acclaim as a great military leader, and the respect and love of people all over the world. And with him, through all the successes and failures, were a loving wife and adoring children and grandchildren.

Ulysses S. Grant had all the failings and virtues of being human. Yet, at the end, his life and his deeds had earned him honor, respect, and love—the true measure of a man's worth.

Bibliography

Catton, Bruce. *Grant Takes Command.* Boston: Little, Brown, 1969. Lincoln's appointment of Grant as supreme commander of all the Union troops gave Grant the opportunity to end the war. This book reveals many of Grant's personal habits, feelings, and strengths.

Catton, Bruce. *U.S. Grant and the American Military Tradition.* Boston: Little, Brown, 1972. A simply written but authentic story of Grant's life, this book is highly recommended. It emphasizes the Civil War and its effect on the general's later life.

Flato, Charles. *The Golden Book of the Civil War.* New York: American Heritage Publishing Co., 1961. This adaptation of the company's adult book has excellent illustrations, photographs, and maps. A good visual reference for students interested in the Civil War and Grant's role in it.

Goldhurst, Richard Crowell. *Many Are the Hearts: The Agony and Triumph of U.S. Grant.* New York: Crowell, 1975. This biography pays particular attention to the last years of Grant's life, especially the writing of his memoirs and his association with Mark Twain. It contains many excellent photographs of Grant and his family.

Grant, Ulysses S. *Personal Memoirs of U.S. Grant.* New York: Da Capo, 1982. This is a condensed version of Grant's autobiography. It contains anecdotes of his childhood, records of his life during the Mexican-American War, and continues until the end of the Civil War.

Kantor, MacKinlay. *Lee and Grant at Appomattox.* New York: Random House, 1950. This book has large print and an easy reading level. It describes the surrender at Appomattox and details the roles of Lee and Grant.

Katz, William Loren. *An Album of the Civil War.* New York: Franklin Watts, 1974. Well illustrated with original prints and photographs, this book also has good sections on Grant and the efforts of black soldiers.

Lewis, Lloyd, *Captain Sam Grant.* Boston: Little Brown, 1950. A delightful study of Grant's early years, this was to be the first part of a two-part biography, but the second part was never written. Considered one of the best records of Grant's years through the Mexican-American War.

McFeeley, William S. *Grant: A Biography.* New York: Norton, 1981. This is one of the most recent and complete biographies of Grant. It earned the author a Pulitzer Prize.

Meyer, Howard N. *Let Us Have Peace: The Story of Ulysses S. Grant.* New York: Collier Books, 1966. This is one of the best books written about Grant for a school-age audience. It highlights Grant's efforts to help the blacks.

Index